CABLE CONFIDENCE

CABLE CONFIDENCE
A GUIDE TO TEXTURED KNITTING

SARA LOUISE HARPER

Martingale®
& COMPANY

CREDITS

President & CEO—Tom Wierzbicki

Publisher—Jane Hamada

Editorial Director—Mary V. Green

Managing Editor—Tina Cook

Technical Editor—Ursula Reikes

Copy Editor—Kathleen Cubley

Design Director—Stan Green

Production Manager—Regina Girard

Illustrator—Robin Strobel

Cover & Text Designer—Shelly Garrison

Photographer—Brent Kane

MISSION STATEMENT

Dedicated to providing quality products
and service to inspire creativity.

Cable Confidence: A Guide to
Textured Knitting
© 2008 by Sara Louise Harper

Martingale®
& COMPANY

Martingale & Company®
20205 144th Ave. NE
Woodinville, WA 98072-8478 USA
www.martingale-pub.com

Printed in China
13 12 11 10 09 08   8 7 6 5 4 3 2 1

**Library of Congress Cataloging-in-
Publication Data is available upon
request.**

ISBN: 978-1-56477-818-5

ACKNOWLEDGMENTS

I have many people to thank for helping me turn my beloved hobby into a livelihood. First and foremost, thank you to my mother, Jane Greer, who taught me to knit in the first place. You can see an example of her handiwork in the Bridget Scarf. I will always treasure the help you have given me and the patience you have shown when the dropped stitches in life were all I could see.

Many thanks to my family who patiently waited until I finished "just one more row" countless times. Thank you Steve, Nicholas, Emily, and Leslie for also willingly trying on sweaters and putting up with samples draped all over the house!

Thank you to Martingale & Company and all the fine editors, illustrators, and photographers who made this book a reality.

Lastly, I am grateful for the wonderful yarn companies who have supplied me with excellent yarns over the years—especially Classic Elite Yarns, with whom I got my start in the knitting world as a sample knitter.

CONTENTS

INTRODUCTION

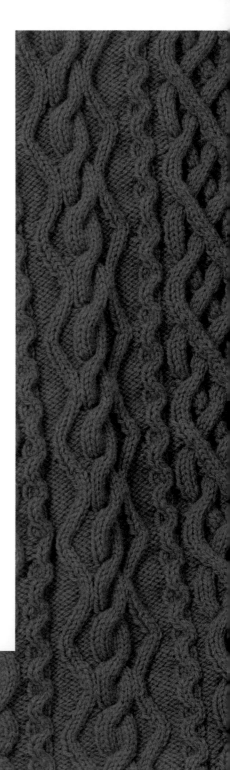

Textured knitting opens up a whole world of creativity and design. You may feel that your skills are not advanced enough to begin textured, or cable, knitting—but you really can do it! Don't be hesitant to try. Cables are not difficult to do once you understand that they are merely stitches worked out of order. Grab a cable needle and see what you can create.

Cable Confidence covers the basics of textured knitting, from the simplest raised elements to the most elaborate of Aran sweaters. You will learn how to read the all-important cable chart, how to work a cable with the aid of a cable needle, and how to incorporate more than one cabled element into a garment.

After you have delved into the world of texture, explore the Aran Islands to see how the famous fishermen's knit sweaters got their start and what makes a sweater an Aran sweater.

This book contains wonderful projects for all levels of knitters—practice your cables by making a throw pillow or a tote bag, then advance from easy textured sweaters to Aran sweaters designed for children, women, or men.

Textured knitting requires all of the standard tools and employs many of the standard methods used for all knitting. Textured knitting is not complex. It does, however, require concentration and attention.

TOOLS

Fill a knitting basket with the items that you will need for your project, including wound yarn, working instructions, and notions (like buttons). Always keep a smaller bag handy, filled with the following knitting accessories: tape measure, crochet hook, scissors, coilless safety pins, stitch holders, stitch markers, row counters, a tapestry needle, and a calculator.

In addition to the tools mentioned above, you will also need one more important tool—a cable needle.

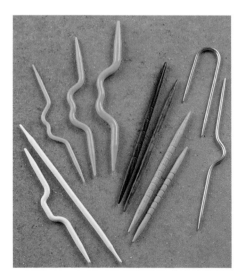

This is a small tool, usually 3½" to 4" long, available in aluminum, plastic, wood, or bamboo, and its sole purpose is to hold a few stitches either to the front or back of the work in order to rearrange the stitch order. It can be straight, hooked, or bird winged, and usually comes in a

package of two or three sizes. Use a cable needle the same size as the project's knitting needles or smaller; a size larger than the knitting needles might stretch out the cabled stitches. Many people advocate cabling without a cable needle because they find it faster and they don't need to worry about losing their cable needle, but I strongly recommend that you use a cable needle—especially when learning. Your stitches will be more uniform and there is far less chance of dropping stitches.

Another useful tool is a magnetic board. Available in several sizes, I find the 8" x 10" size convenient. Made of metal, a magnetic board allows you to use charts with the security of knowing that the magnets will adhere to the proper rows. If you are interrupted mid-row, there is no guesswork as to the pattern row you are working on when you return to your knitting. Numerous patterns can be worked at the same time by using individual magnets on separate charts, and then moving them at the end of each row. Using a magnetic board lets you keep your focus on the knitting where it belongs, and not on fumbling through disorganized instructions.

FIBERS

Wool is commonly known as the fiber that comes from sheep, but it is actually hair from any number of domesticated animals. It is the most traditional fiber to use when working with textured knits because it is strong and flexible. It is tough, resists wrinkles, and bounces back after it gets wet. Wool is also quite soil resistant, which means there will be less care needed to keep it looking great.

Wool is made up of a series of overlapping scales that hold in air and prevent compacting. When worked in a textured design, insulation is compounded because even more air is held where stitches overlap each other. As tough as wool is, though, caution must be used because those same scales that help insulation can also become felted, or locked together, when they come in contact with friction and moisture in varying temperatures. To keep your work looking its best, always follow the care instructions listed on the yarn label.

Wool shows stitches very well, which is another reason it is so popular with cable enthusiasts. Wool blended with mohair or other fuzzy fibers can dull the look of the texture, but this can be a wonderful look in itself—just don't expect too much stitch definition.

There are times, however, when wool isn't the best choice for textured projects. People allergic to wool need to make substitutions. For those with wool allergies, there are other fibers that are suitable for textured knitting. If you need to launder garments frequently or if you live in a warm climate, you may need an alternate fiber. The most common alternatives are acrylic and cotton. Knitters can also find yarn made from bamboo, corn, and soy! Cotton can certainly be used for textured stitching; however, it lacks the elasticity and gentle feel that wool has. With the weight involved in cabled knitting, cotton garments may become extremely elongated over time. There are also some great silks, linens, and blends to choose from, so experiment and find the fiber that best suits your needs.

KNITTING YOUR SWATCH

Swatching is an important aspect of knitting, but many people either don't know why swatches are important or feel they don't need to take the time to knit them. I read once of a knitter who disliked working swatches so much that she always had her mother do them for her!

Swatches are small pieces of knitted fabric, at least 4" x 4", that allow the knitter to become familiar with the stitch pattern that will be worked in the garment. Swatches also allow the knitter to see what the stitch pattern will look like when knit in a certain yarn. Most importantly, though, the swatch measures the size (or gauge) of the knitting so that whichever size you choose to knit, the garment will fit when it is done.

Knitting a swatch *will* save you time in the long run. You will be able to see if your pattern is working with your yarn choice and needle size, and you will become familiar with the pattern being worked—think of it as a practice piece. If the gauge in a pattern is worked in stockinette stitch, I recommend that you also swatch the cable pattern used in the design. Some knitters work stockinette stitch quite loosely, but really tighten up when crossing cables. In textured knitting, the pattern-stitch gauge is much more important than the stockinette-stitch gauge, which may not even be used in the design.

Knitting swatches is a nice habit to get into, and these swatches can be saved for a variety of uses. They can be added on as pockets (outside or inside), they can be used to test laundering or blocking treatments, they can be used in a memory book to document all your knitting forays, or they can be held onto for incorporating into another project like a sampler afghan. If you plan on knitting large swatches, be sure to buy one extra skein of yarn so that you will not run short for your project.

BLOCKING YOUR SWATCH

Blocking your swatch is just as important to the quality of the finished product as making the swatch. Textured swatches, like all gauge swatches, must be treated gently and never stretched or pulled out of shape. When the finished project is blocked you can do more shaping, but a gauge swatch needs an accurate measurement of stitch size.

Using rustproof T-pins, carefully pin the swatch on a flat, padded surface. Record the number of stitches and rows the swatch contains. Next, use a squirt bottle to thoroughly wet the piece. Leave the blocked swatch alone until all is completely dry; then remove the pins.

To measure the swatch, it is best to use a hard ruler. Record the dimensions of the swatch, and then divide the number of stitches by the width measurement and divide the number of rows by the length measurement to arrive at a gauge measurement.

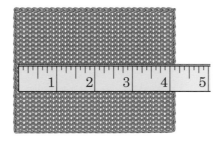

Alternatively, you can use pins to mark 4" in width and length and then count the number of stitches between the pins. Whichever method you use, check the measurements in several areas to be sure of accuracy.

If your first gauge turns out to be too large, you are not getting enough stitches per inch and you must go down a needle size or two and try again. Similarly, if your gauge is too small, or has too many stitches per inch, go up a needle size or two until you find the size that is right for you. If you don't get the same gauge as the designer, you are not doing anything wrong; you just have to make adjustments to your needle size in order to arrive at the gauge in the pattern instructions.

READING INSTRUCTIONS

Knitting has its own language filled with abbreviations. Before you begin a project, please be sure to read and familiarize yourself with any abbreviations used in the pattern. Read through any "Pattern Notes" and check which supplies are needed.

In this book, most patterns are written for the smallest garment size, with larger sizes in parentheses. In some of the more complex projects, the instructions for different garment sizes are written out individually. Always be sure to scan your pattern before starting so that you don't overlook any important information.

READING CHARTS

So many knitters are intimidated by charts or simply avoid charted patterns, which keeps them from knitting great patterns that are only available with charted instructions. A knitting chart is actually a wonderful tool for the knitter. It condenses countless pages of text into an easy-to-read form of knitting shorthand. In fact, many foreign-language patterns can be followed simply because they utilize charts. If you are knitting anything other than garter or stockinette stitch, a chart is a great way to simplify instructions and help you keep track of your pattern row.

Charts are representations of the right side of the knitted fabric, so with one glance at a chart, you know precisely what you need to do next. For example, if you look at a chart in this book and see all white squares, you know that you are working in stockinette stitch. If, on the other hand, you see a cable crossing or a bobble stitch, you know that this is a row where you need to do a specific technique. This is so much easier and faster than having to read a row of text, or in the case of an Aran sweater, many rows of text that often are spread over several pages.

I place the chart on my lap so that I can glance at it while knitting, and I find that I spend very little time studying instructions between rows. For the most part, on the wrong side of the work, textured knitting involves knitting the knits and purling the purls as they are presented; with a chart you can see this instantly. With text instructions, you need to read through an entire line or more just to find out this same information.

There are several types of charting symbols, so always consult the stitch key before starting to knit a pattern. The purpose of the symbols is to convert text instructions into an easy-to-understand form. I find that the easiest type of chart starts with stockinette stitch as the base, shown as a white square, and any deviations from stockinette stitch are shown with lines, shading, or symbols. In other books or magazines, you may find charts that show stockinette stitch as a vertical dash or even a shaded square; you may find charts that depict reverse stockinette stitch as a horizontal dash, a dot, or a shaded square. Thus, it is vital to take the time to read through the stitch key.

Each square in a chart represents one stitch, and each row of a chart represents one row of knitting. All rows are numbered, although the numbers are not always printed. The right side of the work, also known as the public side, is numbered on the right edge of the chart, and rows are read from right to left. The wrong side rows are numbered on the left side of the chart and are read from left to right. Most charts begin with row 1 as a right-side row, but you may find charts that begin with row 1 as a wrong-side row, so the odd-numbered rows appear on the left. Sometimes you may need to work a row or two in order to get the main pattern started; these rows are marked as the foundation rows, and are only worked once. Stitch operations, such as a cable crossing or a bobble, will cover as many squares as there are stitches necessary for the operation. For example, a bobble will cover one square, whereas a four-stitch cable will cover four squares.

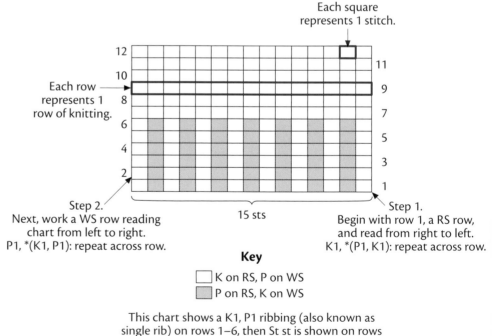

Each square represents 1 stitch.

Each row represents 1 row of knitting.

12 10 8 6 4 2

11 9 7 5 3 1

Step 2.
Next, work a WS row reading chart from left to right.
P1, *(K1, P1): repeat across row.

15 sts

Step 1.
Begin with row 1, a RS row, and read from right to left.
K1, *(P1, K1): repeat across row.

Key

☐ K on RS, P on WS
▨ P on RS, K on WS

This chart shows a K1, P1 ribbing (also known as single rib) on rows 1–6, then St st is shown on rows 7–12. 15 sts are worked for a total of 12 rows.

Charts are read from bottom to top; once you have reached the last row of the chart you return to the bottom and start over. Again, I think that the easiest way to keep your place on the chart is to use an 8" x 10" magnetic board (available at yarn shops). Some knitters like to use sticky notes or pencil marks to keep their places, but sticky notes can fall off over time and pencil marks can confuse you after you've repeated the charts numerous times. Magnetic boards will keep all your charts neat and at hand. I place my board and pattern chart in a plastic protector, so if I want to make notes I can do so with an erasable marker. For example, I can mark on which row sleeve increases should be done and I can also make a notation as to which row a bind off was worked so that I can make the matching piece exactly the same. My chart remains unmarked and clean.

Place the magnet above the row that is being worked. When you follow the rows up as you work, you move the magnets up as well. In this way, you see only the rows on the chart that you have already worked, just as you see only the rows on your needle that you have already knit.

Some people find it easier to keep track of symbols within the charts by color-coding them. The chart for the Robin Pullover (page 55) is an example of identifying stitch actions by color. On this particular chart, the right cross appears in yellow, the left cross appears in blue, and the bobble stitch appears in pink. This is the only color chart in the book; some knitters do not like color in charts because color does not photocopy well (remember, copy charts only for working purposes—never violate copyright laws). Try the color chart

and see how you like it. To make your own, make a photocopy of the desired chart and color code your own symbols using a colored pencil or highlighter.

Allover designs have only one chart to follow; however, the chart sometimes will have its oddities. The chart in the Fiona Vest (page 47) is an example of a chart that does not lie within a perfect rectangle. Rows 3–7 are bumped 2 stitches to the left. There are still 16 repeating stitches, but to keep the pattern correct, the placement of these 16 stitches moves 2 stitches to the left and thus alters the placement of the bold lines. You still follow the chart as before: work the beginning plus stitches, then the 16-stitch repeat across the row, then the ending plus stitches. As with most instructions, if you look at the big picture it is sometimes confusing, but if you follow along one row at a time your pattern will fall into place and you will be amazed at what you can produce.

The easiest way to get used to working with charts is to simply begin. The first two projects in the book, the Alastair Pullover (page 25) and the Bridget Pullover (page 29), include written instructions for the patterns as well as charts. Work with these written instructions by your side so you can double-check that you are on course. It is completely normal to question yourself the first time you knit from a chart. Most people new to charts just need a bit of practice. You may find that the more you work with charts, the less you will want to work with written text. You may become so relaxed with charts that the next time you see pages and pages of written text, you will wonder how you ever finished anything.

WORKING WITH MULTIPLE CHARTS AT ONCE

When faced with many charts to work all at once, attach them all to a magnetic board and place individual magnets on each chart. To further simplify, copy the charts, cut them out, and attach them to a piece of paper in the order in which they will be worked. As each row is completed, move all the magnets at once. If charts need to be spread over two pages, attach the charts to each side of the magnetic board and move the magnets one row every time the board is flipped over. Magnets come in a variety of strengths, so be sure to use strong ones that will not move when the reverse side of the board is in use.

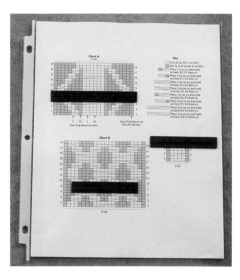

Tip: To help keep track of your place when working with multiple patterns at once, place stitch markers on your needles between patterns. These will be helpful particularly during the first few rows of knitting before the individual patterns have established their beauty.

TEXTURED KNITTING

Texture is commonly defined as a structure of interwoven fibers or other elements. Certainly any knitting that weaves back and forth, like a cable, is considered texture. I also consider knitting that is raised above the knitting surface to be textured. Almost any knitting pattern other than stockinette stitch can be considered textured.

Knitting consists of forming two stitches—when yarn is held to the back of the work, a knit stitch is formed. When yarn is held to the front of the work, a purl stitch is formed. If you are looking at this book, most likely you already know how to do these two stitches. But have you ever thought of working stitches out of order? Wouldn't it be fun to move stitches over and under each other in new and creative ways? That is all textured knitting is—manipulating stitches so that they obtain depth and movement.

All beginning knitters who can knit and purl can work in texture—they just may not realize it. Cables are not nearly as complicated as they seem; by taking one step at a time, you can build on your skills to progress from simple cables in scarves or hats to the masterpieces known as Aran sweaters.

BASIC CABLES

Basic cables break down into two categories: knits over knits (cables) and knits over purls (twists). The easiest crossings to learn are knits over knits, and these are generally worked on a plain background of purl stitches (reverse stockinette stitch). Classic cables, which separate an even number of stitches in half, are crossed to the right by placing the first half of the stitches on the cable needle (see page 10) at the back of the work, or to the left by placing the first half of the stitches on the cable needle at the front of the work.

As shown below, I like to hold a straight cable needle in my right hand under my pinky on rows that contain cable crosses. This gives me freedom to knit and hold the cable needle until I need it.

When it is time to place the stitches on the cable needle, I slip them off and hold the left end of the cable needle under my thumb if the cable needle is in front of the work, or under my index finger if the cable needle is at the back of the work. Using this method, the stitches will not slip off the cable needle, and the cable needle does not get in the way of my knitting. Stitches can then be worked directly from the cable needle.

Holding cable needle under thumb at front

Holding cable needle under index finger at back

Note: Instead of knitting directly from the cable needle, you can place the stitches from the cable needle back onto the left needle before they are knit. This is what is easiest for me. I do this with my right hand and then resume knitting. The cable needle remains in my right hand, ready and waiting for the next cable to be worked.

TWO-STITCH CABLES

A very narrow cable consists of two stitches. On a cable crossing row, stitch #1 (the first stitch on the left needle) is placed on the cable needle either to the front or back of the work, depending on which direction you want the cable to twist. Knit stitch #2 (the next stitch on the left needle), and then knit stitch #1 from the cable needle.

When you have gained more experience, you may want to look into working two-stitch cables without a cable needle (see the key in the Dymphna V-Neck Pullover chart, page 35). For now, though, keep your cable needle handy and practice using it. It should become so natural to have it in your hand that you hardly know it's there.

MULTIPLE-STITCH CABLES

A four-stitch classic cable consists of four stitches (two stitches crossed over two stitches) and is generally crossed every fourth row. A six-stitch classic cable consists of six stitches (three stitches crossed over three stitches) and is generally crossed every sixth row. A larger cable consists of eight or more stitches and can be crossed anywhere from every eight to every fourteen rows.

Four-stitch, six-stitch, and eight-stitch cables crossed to the left and right.

Four-Stitch, Right-Crossing Cable

1. Place the next two stitches to be worked from the left needle to the cable needle.

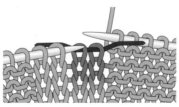

2. Holding the cable needle to the back of the work, knit the next two stitches on the left needle.

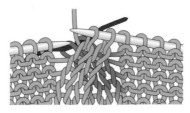

3. Knit the two stitches from the cable needle onto the right needle to finish the right cable cross.

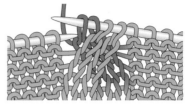

Four-Stitch, Left-Crossing Cable

1. Place two stitches on the cable needle and hold them at the front of the work.

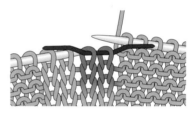

2. Knit the next two stitches from the left needle onto the right needle, leaving the cable needle alone.

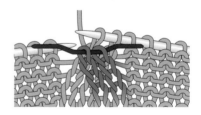

3. Knit the stitches off the cable needle to complete the cable cross to the left.

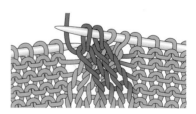

BRAIDS

Braids: from simple to more complex.

Braids consist of a number of stitches that form strands, which are interwoven up the sweater by moving the strands over and under each other. Braids have been used in the Dymphna V-Neck Pullover (page 35), the Emer Pullover (page 59), and the Sinead Pullover (page 63).

Braids take the basic cable one step further by adding in one or more columns of crossing stitches. Where there were two elements in the cable, now there are at least three in the braid. The most familiar braid, a plait, is commonly used in a little girl's hairstyle. The strands in a braid can consist of any number of stitches, but normally contain two or three stitches per strand. A simple braid moves up the knitting in a maintained width. An expansion to that concept forms the more interesting braids, which utilize traveling stitches (discussed at right) that move over several purl stitches before returning to the center to be braided. Using more strands gives you the opportunity to weave the braid in and out, but also increases the difficulty level.

BOBBLES

Bobbles are fun and lend a lot of texture to a design. They can be a variety of sizes, depending on how many stitches are created out of the original stitch. I think the five-stitch bobble is a universal size.

To make a reverse stockinette stitch bobble (Robin Pullover, page 55), work to the desired spot for the bobble, then K1, P1, K1, P1, K1 all in the same stitch. Turn the work and knit these five stitches. Turn the work and purl these five stitches. Then pass the second, third, fourth, and fifth stitches over the first stitch. Only one stitch remains and the bobble is complete.

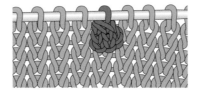

Changing how the five stitches are worked can alter the appearance of the bobbles. For a stockinette-stitch bobble (Trinity Pillow on page 39), after increasing from one stitch to five, turn and purl five stitches; then turn and knit five stitches. For a garter-stitch bobble, turn and knit five stitches; then turn and knit five stitches. Finish each bobble by passing the stitches over until one stitch remains.

DIAMOND CABLES

Diamonds can be filled with reverse stockinette stitch (which makes them appear not to be filled at all), moss stitch, or bobbles.

The diamond cable, which is used frequently in Aran sweaters, crosses knits over purls to form a running line known as a traveling stitch. The center of a traditional diamond contains reverse stockinette stitch, garter stitch, seed stitch, or moss stitch. However, diamonds can be filled with bobbles, leaves, or even embroidery. Diamonds are fun and easy to knit, and you can make them in a variety of sizes. Any errors are easily seen, so you can make corrections immediately. With all the variety that diamonds offer, they never become dull. A diamond cable is worked on the front and back of the Emer Pullover (page 59).

A note about traveling stitches: when crossing knits over purls, remember that the knits must remain in front of the purls in order to be seen. When traveling to the right, the purls will be held to the back of the work; when traveling to the left, the knits will be held to the front of the work. Always follow the chart and consult the stitch key, but with practice you will see the progression of the knit stitches, especially in a pattern such as a diamond, and know at a glance when the stitches should be placed on the cable needle and held to the front or back of the work.

Moving Two Knit Stitches to the Right

1. Place the purl stitch from the left needle onto the cable needle and hold to the back of the work.

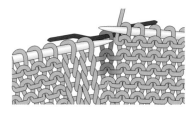

2. Knit the two stitches from the left needle onto the right needle.

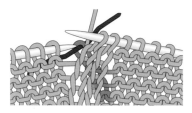

3. Finish by purling the purl stitch held on the cable needle.

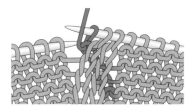

Moving Two Knit Stitches to the Left

1. Place two knit stitches on the cable needle and hold to the front of the work.

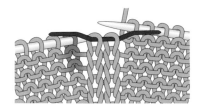

2. Purl the next stitch from the left needle onto the right needle.

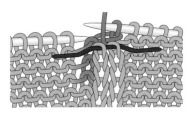

3. Knit the two stitches being held at the front of the work to finish.

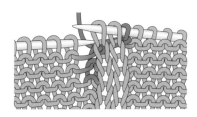

ALTERNATING CABLES

A great way to obtain a textured design is to alternate two different cable patterns. By alternating a showy cable with a subdued cable you can achieve a great textured look that is similar to an Aran sweater design. Alternating a cable with a filler stitch (see page 23) on sleeves will make the knitting a bit easier without losing the overall textured look. You'll see alternating cables in the Skylar Felted Bag (page 51) and the Sinead Pullover (page 63).

CABLE FLARE

Cables, by their nature, pull in the fabric every time they are crossed. Their gauge will differ from the ribbing gauge—sometimes drastically. The puckering that occurs when there are too many stitches in the ribbing when compared with the stitches in the cable is called cable flare. This flaring can occur not only when transitioning from a body or sleeve ribbing to the main cabled pattern, but also when working a ribbed neckline. To more closely match the gauges, many patterns increase the number of stitches when the transition to the cabled area begins. If you are knitting a cable and the flaring is noticeable, remember that the number of stitches in the ribbing can always be reduced and then increased back up at the transition point (either the last row of ribbing or the first row of cable pattern). Try not to work increases evenly across the row unless you're working an allover cable pattern (see page 23). Rather, place the increases at the base of the cables—more stitches for the larger cables and fewer for the smaller ones.

Too many stitches in the ribbing causes severe puckering.

Adjusting the stitch count keeps the piece balanced.

HELPFUL TECHNIQUES

The following techniques were used for many of the projects in this book. Techniques specific to a certain pattern are explained in sidebars within that pattern's instructions.

EDGE STITCHES

Edge stitches are knitted, purled, or slipped stitches at the beginning, end, or both the beginning and end of rows to keep the pattern from becoming distorted at the edges. Less distortion means easier and more expert seaming. There are many different ways to work edge stitches, but I find the easiest is the garter-edge stitch—simply knit the first and last stitch on every row. If you prefer a different edge stitch, by all means use it.

RUSSIAN JOIN

I like to use a Russian join when working with wool on textured knits. More texture is usually found in the middle of rows than on edges, and this type of join helps camouflage woven ends, eliminates the need to join new yarn only at the ends of rows, and is very strong.

As you near the end of your working strand, thread the end in a tapestry needle and weave it back through the plies of yarn as invisibly as possible. Leave a small loop at the end and insert the new yarn into it.

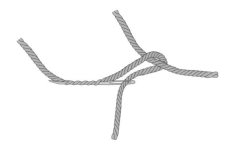

Repeat the process with the new strand so that the two yarns are joined by two loops. Pull gently on each end until the join is as smooth as possible. Clip any yarn still remaining after the loops have been smoothed out.

The Russian join should not be used with a very smooth or treated yarn, such as superwash wool, nor should it be used when the knitting should lay very flat.

BINDING OFF IN PATTERN

Binding off in pattern allows the pattern to continue up through and into the bind-off row. Cables that are bound off in pattern do not stop all at once. They appear to keep going right into the seam of a sweater and give the whole piece a much more professional appearance. On the bind-off row, work the next row of the pattern as if you were *not* binding off—it is like working two steps at the same time. Some people knit the knits and purl the purls as they appear while binding off, but this is not the correct way to approach binding off textured pieces.

When you work a seed-stitch pattern, you work K1, P1, K1, P1 across the row. On the following row, you will purl over the knit stitches and knit over the purl stitches so that the pattern continues in a sort of checkerboard pattern. If you knit over the knits and purl over the purls when

you bind off, you will knit a final row that resembles ribbing and not seed stitch. Likewise, if you were to bind off in all knit stitches, half would be correct and maintain the seed-stitch pattern and the other half would appear as ribbing.

When cable crosses need to be worked on a bind-off row, place the required number of stitches on the cable needle just as you would if you were working an ordinary row. As soon as you have two stitches on the right needle, bind one off. Work the next stitch in the pattern, whether it is from the cable needle or the left needle, and again bind it off. You may need a bit of dexterity, but this will come with practice. Alternatively, you can work the cable crossing and when all the stitches have been crossed and are on the right needle, transfer them back to the left needle one at a time. Bind them off one at a time without working them further.

If you have a cable that is not due to be crossed yet, you may need to decrease the stitches to avoid cable flare. In this case, simply knit two stitches together or purl two stitches together (depending on which stitches are presenting themselves) once or twice within the cable. This will help keep your knitted piece shaped correctly. On larger cables I try to decrease two stitches, one on each end of the cable, and on smaller cables I try to decrease one stitch in the middle of the cable. See what works best on your individual cables and with practice you will be able to decide on the best method, or if a decrease is even necessary.

SEAMING

The mattress stitch is a good all-purpose seaming stitch. Lay the pieces side by side with the right side of the work facing you. Bring the darning needle under the horizontal bar between the first and second stitches on one side, and then bring the needle under the horizontal bar between the first and second stitches directly opposite. For a very narrow seam, work through the centers of the stitches; for a more secure wider seam, bring the needle under the bar between the second and third stitches.

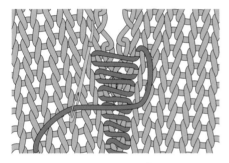

Mattress stitch

In textured and Aran sweaters, a saddle section (a narrow strip of knitting that sits atop the shoulders) is often used to connect the top of the sleeve to the neckband. When sewing shoulder seams or a saddle section to front and back pieces, pin them together carefully to make sure that like cables are directly opposite each other.

Use coilless safety pins to pin the entire sweater together before seaming for an easy, neat, and stable way to ensure smooth seams. Sew from the front side of the work using a mattress stitch. Knitted pieces with a lot of patterning are very forgiving, but it's still important to use good seaming practices. Working under a good light and using a tapestry needle with a bent tip makes seaming easier. Take time to do a really nice job—sweaters are not knit in one sitting, so they needn't be seamed in one sitting.

WEAVING IN YARN ENDS

The more you knit, the more techniques you learn to give you a truly professional look. Taking care of yarn ends is one such technique. When you are casting on stitches, try leaving an extra long tail. This can be used as a seaming yarn and will help you avoid one more yarn end to weave.

Wool, my preferred fiber for cables, is great to weave in because the hairs adhere to each other and help keep it from unraveling. When you are weaving in ends, go through the middle of the yarn at the back of the work so that more hairs can catch on each other. This is not the time to avoid splitting stitches—it will actually help.

Stitches will unravel more easily if they follow a straight line. Try to make it difficult for them by weaving in ends using a duplicate stitch technique on the back of the work.

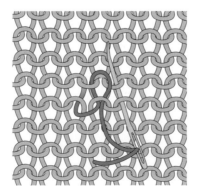

Some people also like to weave their ends in by going up three or four stitches diagonally then turning and coming down three or four stitches next to the first diagonal.

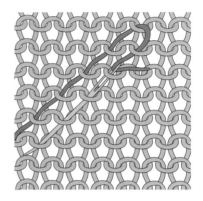

Whichever method you use, make sure that it is secure and does not show from the front of the work.

SINGLE CROCHET

To work a row of single crochet on the edge of a knitted piece:

1. Insert a crochet hook into a stitch on the edge of the knitting and draw a loop through to the front. Wrap the yarn around the hook and draw a second loop through the first to secure.

2. Working from right to left, insert the crochet hook into the next stitch on the edge of the knitting.

3. Pull the working yarn through to the front. Two loops are now on the hook.

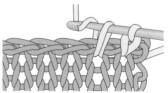

4. Wrap the yarn around the hook and pull through both loops on the hook. One loop remains on the hook.

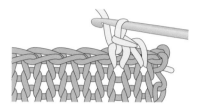

Repeat steps 2–4 around the entire edge.

BLOCKING AND CARING FOR TEXTURED SWEATERS

When you have finished knitting a wool sweater, it will need to be blocked. Lay your sweater out on a flat surface, such as a bed, a table covered with towels, or a blocking board and shape it to the width and length specified on the schematic. Use rustproof T-pins to pin the sweater in place and thoroughly mist the sweater with a spray bottle of water or a steamer. Let the sweater dry completely. Take special care not to flatten the texture when you're blocking your sweater; never iron or overly steam textured knits.

While sweaters require occasional washing, they don't need to be washed after every wearing. Certainly, though, you should wash your wool sweaters at the end of the season before they are stored away. After very gently hand washing the sweater in lukewarm water and a wool wash, place it in a large towel and roll to remove excess water, taking care not to roll too tightly. Wool will felt very easily; too much friction from trying to get the garment dry will begin the felting process, so don't ring out the sweater or rub it with a towel.

I like to wash my sweaters on a nice warm day, and then lay them outside on towels to dry. You will be amazed at how quickly they dry outside. If this is not an option, though, be sure to lay them completely flat because wool will take on the shape of the drying surface. Do not ever hang a sweater to dry, because the sweater may become misshapen and get permanent hanger marks in the shoulder area. Wool sweaters are very strong, but they must be treated delicately when wet.

Sweaters are best kept folded and laid flat. To fold a sweater, lay it down with the back facing up and fold each sleeve straight over the upper back of the sweater. Next, fold the lower back up over the sleeves. Turn it over and you have a nicely folded sweater with only one area that could develop a crease.

Store sweaters where they can receive plenty of air, and never in plastic bags. If you are afraid that moths might be a problem, hang a sachet of lavender or place a piece of cedar nearby. Both are moth deterrents that actually do an amazing job.

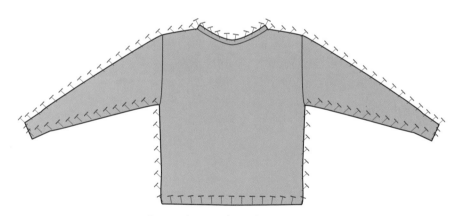

Space pins evenly and generously along the edges of the garment.

THE ARAN SWEATER

Aran sweaters are the masterpieces of textured knitting. They are symmetrically designed sweaters containing cables and are completely patterned over the front, back, and sleeves. The famous Irish sweaters were originally made from the sheep's wool found on the bitter cold, windy, and desolate Aran Islands, which are a group of three islands off the coast of Galway, Ireland. The wool is known as bainin (pronounced "bawneen"), Gaelic for "white" or "undyed," and is the coarse, cream, or oatmeal-colored wool common in Aran sweaters.

No one is certain where the famous Aran stitch patterns first came from, but there are several theories. One theory is that the patterns were derived from the famous *Book of Kells*, but over recent years that theory has become increasingly less believable. After all, how would the Aran Islanders, who were so cut off from the world, ever have seen the *Book of Kells* or known of its existence?

The first knitted Aran sweaters were made between 1900 and 1930, purchased from the Aran Islanders and sold in Dublin to eager tourists. In the late 1930s and early 1940s, Patons Yarns began publishing Aran sweater patterns after being supplied with Aran handknits through Ó'Máille's, a clothing store in Galway, Ireland.

It was sometime after this that the myth developed, as part of an Irish marketing ploy, about the long history of the sweaters, in part to aid in their sales and to call attention to the existence of the Aran Islands. Tourists were told that Aran Islanders were members of clans, and just like the clans of Scotland who had specific tartans, the Aran clans had individual cable patterns, mainly to identify fishermen who perished at sea and washed ashore. This is all an exaggeration of the fact that mothers would pass their knitting knowledge down to their daughters, so some cables became family favorites.

PATTERN MEANINGS

The majority of Aran stitches relate to family and the Aran Islanders' main occupations—fishing and farming. It was a lonely, hard life on the islands, and next to religion, family was of the utmost importance. Basic cables symbolizing ropes and braided patterns symbolizing nets are the mainstay of Aran stitch designs. Also quite popular are diamonds, which symbolize both wealth and the rocky border of the fields; moss stitches, which symbolize the seaweed which fertilized the fields; and honeycombs, which symbolize the hardworking nature of bees. Trinity stitch is a meaningful religious pattern—it symbolizes God in three persons as originally introduced to the Irish by Saint Patrick.

Originally, all patterns were passed down through generations orally. Once the patterns began to be written down and later published, the designs could further be enhanced and shared among knitters worldwide.

SWEATER DESIGNS

Aran pullovers include a strong panel that is usually the largest and most visually stunning pattern in the sweater. Flanking this panel are more subdued patterns. This design is repeated across the sweater, with cables and textured designs alternating in width and difficulty, stopping an inch or two from the side seam. Filler stitch patterns are generally worked here and are usually the plainest of all the patterns. Aran sweaters are knit flat in pieces and then seamed.

Cardigans differ from pullovers only in their lack of a center panel. Each side is a mirror image of the other, and buttons are traditionally wooden or leather.

Knitting Aran sweaters takes time, effort, and concentration, but most people will agree that it is all worth it, and what results from that time and effort is a beautiful, heirloom piece of art.

A beautiful example of an authentic Aran sweater, this cardigan was purchased by the author's grandmother in Dublin, Ireland, around 1970.

Another stitch pattern is worked on the back of the sweater to fill the center area.

MORE TEXTURED PATTERNS

Many different types of patterns are used to create richly textured sweaters.

MOTIFS

Textured patterns can be worked in motifs or allover patterns. The difference between the two is that a motif has a beginning and an end, whereas the allover patterns are worked in multiples of stitches and can go on endlessly. An example of a motif would be the center cable on the Bridget Pullover (page 29). This cable contains eight stitches, so it would be an eight-stitch motif. Similarly, the diamond cable in the Emer Pullover (page 59) is a motif; it has a fixed number of stitches. Many motifs can be knit side by side, but they will not become an allover pattern. One example of a side-by-side motif is the horseshoe cable, often called a double cable, seen in the Nellwyn Cardigan (page 43). It is formed by working a right cable and a left cable next to each other.

Two cables that fall into both classifications are the trinity stitch and honeycomb pattern. Both are composed of side-by-side repeated patterns and can be knit as a motif or an allover pattern. Perhaps their diversity is why they are so popular in textured knitting.

ALLOVER PATTERNS

Allover patterns have a repeated number of stitches (known as a "multiple"), plus they can have a certain number of stitches that lead into or out of the design, or they can have edge stitches. For example the trinity stitch pattern at right is a multiple of four stitches plus two, which in this instance are edge stitches. To knit a piece containing five multiples of pattern, for example, you would multiply the "multiple" number of stitches by the number of pattern repeats needed, then add the "plus" number, which will only be worked once. For the trinity stitch, 4 stitches x 5 repeats = 20 stitches; plus 2 stitches = 22 stitches needed for 5 repeats.

Knowing your gauge measurement, you can calculate how many multiples of pattern it will take to get to a desired measurement. For example, if your gauge is 5 stitches per inch and you want to make a pillow 14" wide, multiply 5 stitches x 14", which is 70 stitches. If your pattern is a multiple of 4 stitches plus 2, subtract the plus 2 stitches, then divide this number, 68, by the number of multiples. This must be a round number, so any adjustments must be made here. In our example, 68 divided by 4 = 17, so 70 stitches should be cast on. Knowing how to perform these calculations will enable you to make pillows or afghans of any size with any pattern you desire.

FILLER STITCHES

A filler stitch is a stitch pattern in its own right and is beautiful enough to pattern an entire sweater. Most filler stitches have a great deal of texture, although they're generally not worked with a cable needle. Filler stitches calm down the design and allow each element to be seen and appreciated.

Examples of classic filler stitches include garter stitch, seed stitch, and moss stitch. However, any knit and purl pattern can be used. The Dymphna V-Neck Pullover (page 35) shows how beautiful and complex a design can be when using filler stitches like moss stitch and a basket weave pattern. There is only one braid cable in the entire sweater, yet because of the texture of the filler stitch patterns, it reads as a highly textured, Aran-looking pullover.

Trinity Stitch

The trinity stitch can be tricky because the pattern is worked on the wrong side of the work. You will purl on the right side of rows 1 and 3. On wrong-side rows, you make three stitches out of one by working a (K1, P1, K1) all into the same stitch and then purl three stitches together.

Multiple of 4 sts + 2.

Row 1 (RS): K1 (edge st), purl across to last st, K1 (edge st).

Row 2: K1, *(K1, P1, K1) into same st, P3tog; rep from *, K1.

Row 3: K1 (edge st), purl across to last st, K1 (edge st).

Row 4: K1, *P3tog, (K1, P1, K1) into same st; rep from *, K1.

ALASTAIR PULLOVER

The simplicity of this design makes it perfect for men and for women. Three cables grouped together give this sweater design interest.

Skill Level: Easy ◼◼☐☐

Unisex Sizes:
Extra Small (Small, Medium, Large)

Finished Chest: 36 (40, 44, 48)"

Finished Length: 24 (25, 26, 27)"

MATERIALS

14 (16, 18, 20) balls of Plymouth Tweed from Plymouth Yarns (100% lambs wool; 50 g; 109 yds) in color 5459 ⒋

US 7 (4.5 mm) circular needle (24" long) or size required for gauge

Cable needle

Stitch holders

Tapestry needle

GAUGE

18 sts and 28 rows = 4" in St st

23 sts and 28 rows = 4" in cable panel

Always work a gauge swatch to ensure proper fit.

CABLE PANEL ⟨CHART⟩

Follow text below or chart on page 27.

(Worked over 26 sts)

Rows 1, 5, 7, 9 (RS): P2, *K6, P2; rep from * twice.

Rows 2, 4, 6, 8: K2, *P6, K2; rep from * twice.

Row 3: P2, *place 3 sts on cn and hold at back; K3, K3 from cn, P2; rep from * twice.

Row 10: K2, *P6, K2; rep from * twice.

Rep rows 1–10 for patt.

BACK

CO 94 (102, 110, 118) sts and work in K2, P2 ribbing until piece measures 2" from CO edge, ending with WS row.

Beg main patt as follows, working row 1 of chart: Work 4 (6, 7, 8) sts in St st; work chart inc 2 sts evenly; *work 7 (10, 13, 16) sts in St st; work chart inc 2 (3, 3, 3) sts evenly; rep from * once; work 4 (6, 7, 8) sts in St st—100 (110, 118, 126) sts.

Work in est patt until piece measures 24 (25, 26, 27)" from CO edge. BO all sts in patt.

FRONT

Work as for back until piece measures 21 (22, 23, 24)" from CO edge, ending with WS row.

Neck shaping: Work 41 (43, 46, 49) sts, attach a new ball of yarn and BO center 18 (24, 26, 28) sts, work rem sts. Dec 2 sts at each neck edge EOR 4 times—33 (35, 38, 41) sts for each shoulder.

Work even on each side until piece measures same as back. BO all sts in patt.

SLEEVES ⟨MAKE 2⟩

CO 40 (44, 46, 48) sts and work in K2, P2 ribbing for 2", ending with WS row.

Beg main patt as follows, working row 1 of chart: work 7 (9, 10, 11) sts in St st; work chart; work 7 (9, 10, 11) sts in St st. AT THE SAME TIME inc 1 st at each end EOR 4 (0, 4, 5) times, then every 5 rows 19 (23, 22, 24) times—86 (90, 98, 106) sts; work incs in St st.

Work even until piece measures 18 (20, 21, 21)" from CO edge, ending with WS row.

Saddle: BO 38 (40, 44, 48) sts; work 2 sts in rev St st; work 1 cable as est over 6 sts, work 2 sts in rev St st; work to end. On next row, BO 38 (40, 44, 48) sts and work rem 10 sts as est until saddle measures approx 6 (6½, 7, 7¾)". Place sts on holder.

FINISHING

Sew saddle sections between back and front pieces, adjusting length as necessary. Place pins 9 (9½, 10, 11)" from midpoint of saddle and sew sleeves between pins. Sew sleeve and side seams.

Neckband: K10 from left front holder, PU 16 (18, 20, 20) sts down left front, PU 20 (22, 24, 26) sts across front, PU 16 (18, 20, 20) sts up right front, K10 from holder, PU 32 (34, 36, 42) sts across back—104 (112, 120, 128) sts. Work in K2, P2 ribbing until neckband measures 1½" or desired length. BO loosely in patt.

Weave in all loose ends. Block gently, being careful not to crush texture or distort ribbing.

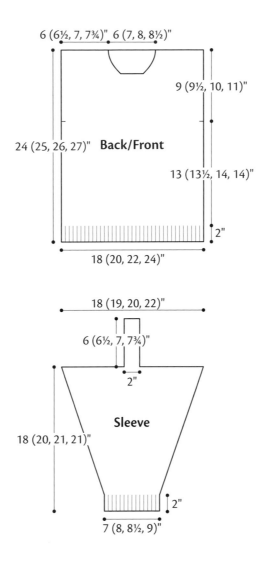

6 (6½, 7, 7¾)" 6 (7, 8, 8½)"

9 (9½, 10, 11)"

Back/Front

24 (25, 26, 27)"

13 (13½, 14, 14)"

2"

18 (20, 22, 24)"

18 (19, 20, 22)"

6 (6½, 7, 7¾)"

2"

Sleeve

18 (20, 21, 21)"

2"

7 (8, 8½, 9)"

Chart

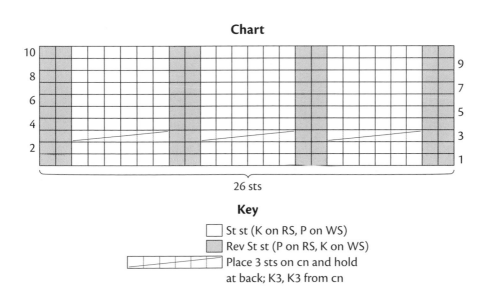

10

8

6

4

2

9

7

5

3

1

26 sts

Key

□ St st (K on RS, P on WS)

▨ Rev St st (P on RS, K on WS)

▨ Place 3 sts on cn and hold
at back; K3, K3 from cn

BRIDGET PULLOVER

This is a great, simple look for children of all ages.
The neckline on this sweater has a fun, V-notch edge.

Skill Level: Easy ■■□□

Children's Sizes: 4 (6, 8, 10, 12)

Finished Chest: 26 (28, 30, 32, 36)"

Finished Length: 16 (18, 18, 19, 20)"

MATERIALS

7 (8, 9, 10, 11) balls of Duchess from
Classic Elite Yarns (40% merino, 28%
viscose, 15% nylon, 10% cashmere,
7% angora; 50 g; 75 yds) in color
1003 Genteel Grey

US 9 (5.5 mm) needles

US 10.5 (6.5 mm) needles or size
required for gauge

Size G/6 (4 mm) crochet hook

Cable needle

Tapestry needle

GAUGE

18 sts and 19 rows = 4" in K2, P2
ribbing on larger needles

Always work a gauge swatch to
ensure proper fit.

CABLE PANEL

Follow text below or chart A on page
31.

(Worked over 12 sts)

**Rows 1, 3, 5, 7, 19, 21, 23, 25, 27
(RS):** P2, K3, P2, K3, P2.

Rows 2, 4, 6, 8, 18, 20, 22, 24, 26: K2,
P3, K2, P3, K2.

Row 9: P2, sl 4 sts to cn and hold at
front; K4, K4 from cn, P2.

Rows 11, 13, 15: P2, K8, P2.

Row 10, 12, 14, 16: K2, P8, K2.

Row 17: P2, sl 4 sts to cn and hold at
front; K3, P1; P1, K3 from cn, P2.

Row 28: K2, P3, K2, P3, K2.

Rep rows 1–28 for patt.

BACK

Using smaller needles, CO 58 (66,
70, 74, 82) sts. Set up ribbing as
follows:

Row 1: K1 (edge st); work 18 (22, 22,
26, 30) sts using chart B; work 4 (4, 6,
4, 4) sts in rev St st; work 12 sts using
chart A; work 4 (4, 6, 4, 4) sts in rev
St st; work 18 (22, 22, 26, 30) sts
using chart B; K1 (edge stitch).

Row 2: K1, knit the knit sts and purl
the purl the purl sts as they face you,
end with K1.

Rep last 2 rows twice more for
ribbing.

Change to larger needles.

Work in est patt beg on row 1 of
chart A until piece measures 10 (11½,
11½, 12½, 12¾)" from CO edge.

Armhole shaping: BO 6 sts at beg of
next 2 rows—46 (54, 58, 62, 70) sts.

Work even in est patt until piece
measures 6 (6½, 6½, 6½, 7¼)" from
armhole BO, ending with WS row.

Neck shaping: On next row, work 18
(22, 23, 24, 27) sts in est patt, attach
a new ball of yarn and BO center 10
(10, 12, 14, 16) sts, work rem sts. At
each neck edge, BO 3 sts on next 2
rows—12 (16, 17, 18, 21) sts for each
shoulder. On next row, BO all sts in
patt.

FRONT

Work as for back until piece measures 3½ (3½, 4, 4, 4½)" from armhole BO, ending with WS row.

Neck shaping: Work 23 (27, 29, 31, 35) sts, attach a new ball of yarn and work rem sts. Working each side separately, work 8 rows even, then at each neck edge, BO 3 sts twice, BO 2 sts 2 (2, 3, 3, 4) times, BO 1 (1, 0, 1, 0) st once—12 (16, 17, 18, 21) sts for each shoulder.

Work even on each side to same length as back. BO all sts in patt.

SLEEVES ⟨MAKE 2⟩

Using smaller needles, CO 30 (30, 34, 34, 34) sts and work in K2, P2 ribbing for 6 rows. Change to larger needles and cont in K2, P2 ribbing, inc 1 st at each end on next and every 3 (3, 3, 4, 3) rows for a total of 12 (14, 12, 12, 16) times—54 (58, 58, 58, 66) sts. Work even until piece measures 12 (13, 14, 15, 17)" from CO edge, or desired length. BO all sts in patt.

FINISHING

Sew shoulders tog. Pin sleeves in armhole area and sew. Sew sleeve and side seams.

Edging: Using crochet hook, work 1 row of sc around neckline, bottom edge of sweater, and edges of sleeves. See "Single Crochet" on page 19.

Weave in all loose ends. Block gently, being careful not to crush texture.

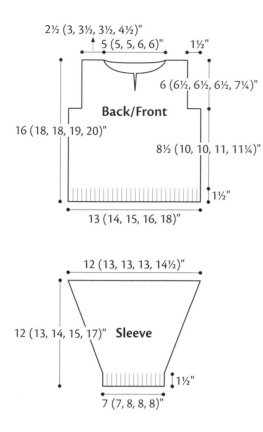

2½ (3, 3½, 3½, 4½)"

↑ 5 (5, 5, 6, 6)"   1½"

6 (6½, 6½, 6½, 7¼)"

Back/Front

16 (18, 18, 19, 20)"

8½ (10, 10, 11, 11¼)"

1½"

13 (14, 15, 16, 18)"

12 (13, 13, 13, 14½)"

12 (13, 14, 15, 17)" **Sleeve**

1½"

7 (7, 8, 8, 8)"

Chart A

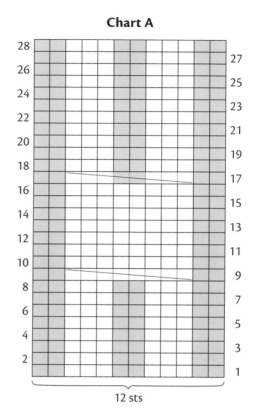

12 sts

Chart B
K2, P2 ribbing

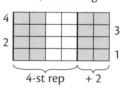

4-st rep   + 2

Key

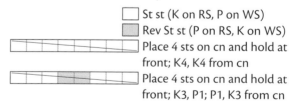

☐ St st (K on RS, P on WS)

▨ Rev St st (P on RS, K on WS)

Place 4 sts on cn and hold at front; K4, K4 from cn

Place 4 sts on cn and hold at front; K3, P1; P1, K3 from cn

BRIDGET SCARF

The long length of this scarf makes it
very versatile for kids as well as adults.

Skill Level: Easy ◼◼☐☐

One Size: Approx 3½" x 90"

MATERIALS

3 balls of Princess from Classic Elite
Yarns (40% merino, 28% viscose,
15% nylon, 10% cashmere, 7%
angora; 50 g; 150 yds) in color 3419
Precious Pink ⓷

US 7 (4.5 mm) needles or size
required for gauge

Cable needle

Tapestry needle

GAUGE

24 sts and 24 rows = 4" in K2, P2
ribbing

Always work a gauge swatch.

BRIDGET SCARF

CO 30 sts and work in K2, P2
ribbing for 6 rows.

Beg main patt as follows, working
row 1 of the charts on page 31. K1
(edge st), work 8 sts using chart B;
work chart A; work 8 sts using chart
B; K1 (edge st).

Work in est patt until scarf measures
approx 89" or desired length. Work
K2, P2 ribbing for 6 rows. BO all sts
in patt. Weave in all ends, then block
gently.

Dymphna V-Neck Pullover

This pullover contains great texture and looks much more difficult than it really is.

Skill Level: Intermediate ◼◼◼◻

Women's Sizes: Small (Medium, Large, Extra Large)

Finished Chest: 40 (44, 48, 52)"

Finished Length: 25 (26, 27, 28)"

MATERIALS

12 (14, 16, 18) hanks of Renaissance from Classic Elite Yarns (100% wool; 50 g; 110 yds) in color 7102 Sicilian Sun (4)

US 8 (5 mm) needles or size required for gauge

US 8 (5 mm) circular needle (32" long) for neckband

Cable needle

Tapestry needle

GAUGE

21 sts and 28 rows = 4" in moss patt

Always work a gauge swatch to ensure proper fit.

BACK

CO 112 (116, 124, 132) sts and work 12 rows using Chart D.

Beg main patt as follows, working row 1 of charts, and inc 2 (5, 7, 6) sts evenly in first row: K1 (edge st); work 23 (23, 28, 35) sts using chart A; work chart B; work chart C 4 (5, 5, 4) times; work chart B; work 23 (23, 28, 35) sts using chart A; K1 (edge st)—114 (121, 131, 138) sts.

Work in est patt until piece measures 16 (16, 17, 17)" from CO edge, ending with a WS row.

Armhole shaping: BO 10 (10, 10, 14) sts beg of next 2 rows—94 (101, 111, 110) sts. Work even in est patt until piece measures 8¾ (9¾, 9¾, 10¾)" from armhole BO, ending with WS row.

Neck shaping: Work in est patt across 34 (35, 38, 35) sts, attach a new ball of yarn and BO center 26 (31, 35, 40) sts, work rem sts.

Work even in est patt for 2 rows. BO all sts in patt.

FRONT

Work as for back until piece measures 16 (16, 17, 17)" from CO edge, ending with a WS row.

Armhole and neck shaping: On next row, BO 10 (10, 10, 14) sts; work in est patt across 46 (50, 55, 55) sts; BO 2 (1, 1, 0) sts; attach a new ball of yarn and work rem sts. At beg of next row, BO 10 (10, 10, 14) sts, then work across row in est patt using separate balls of yarn for each side of V neck. Work in est patt, dec 1 st at each neck edge EOR 26 (28, 31, 30) as follows: work to 3 sts before neck separation, K2tog, K1; after neck separation K1, ssk, work to end of row. Maintaining garter st edge on each side of neck separation, work even on 20 (22, 24, 25) sts until each side measures same as back. BO all sts in patt.

SLEEVES ⟨MAKE 2⟩

CO 42 (42, 54, 54) sts and work 12 rows using chart D (omit edge sts). On next row, work all sts using chart A, inc 1 st each end EOR 0 (7, 0, 7) times, then every 4 rows 26 (20, 25, 24) times—94 (96, 104, 116) sts.

Work even until sleeve measures 18 (19, 20, 21)" from CO edge, or desired length. BO all sts in patt.

FINISHING

Sew shoulders tog. Pin sleeves in armhole area and sew. Sew sleeve and side seams.

V-neck edging: Using circular needle and beg at base of V neck, PU 166 (182, 198, 214) sts evenly around neck edge. Working back and forth in rows, K1 (edge st), work 4-st rep of chart D beg on row 2 (WS), K1 (edge st). When ribbing measures 1" or desired length, BO all sts in patt. Tack one end of ribbing to inside and one end of ribbing to outside of neckline.

Weave in all ends. Block gently, being careful not to crush texture.

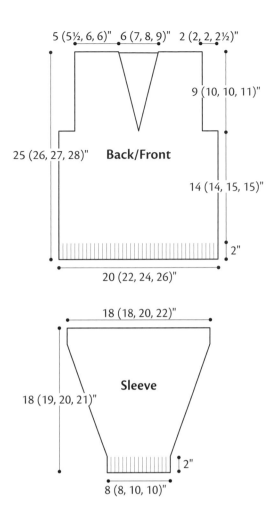

5 (5½, 6, 6)"   6 (7, 8, 9)"   2 (2, 2, 2½)"

9 (10, 10, 11)"

Back/Front

25 (26, 27, 28)"

14 (14, 15, 15)"

2"

20 (22, 24, 26)"

18 (18, 20, 22)"

Sleeve

18 (19, 20, 21)"

2"

8 (8, 10, 10)"

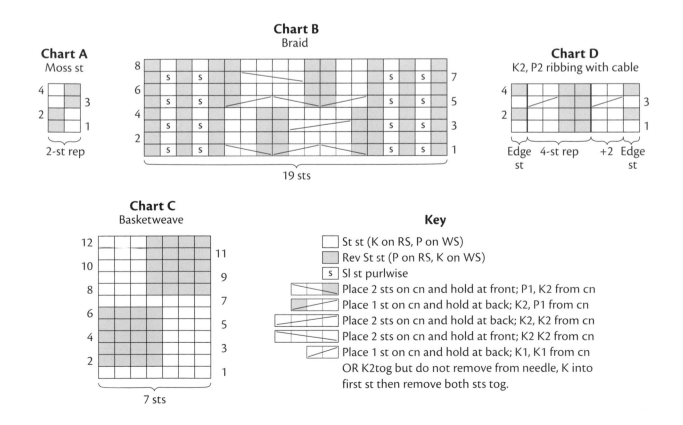

Chart A
Moss st

4
2
3
1

2-st rep

Chart B
Braid

8
6
4
2

7
5
3
1

19 sts

Chart D
K2, P2 ribbing with cable

4
2
3
1

Edge st   4-st rep   +2   Edge st

Chart C
Basketweave

12
10
8
6
4
2

11
9
7
5
3
1

7 sts

Key

☐ St st (K on RS, P on WS)

▨ Rev St st (P on RS, K on WS)

s Sl st purlwise

Place 2 sts on cn and hold at front; P1, K2 from cn

Place 1 st on cn and hold at back; K2, P1 from cn

Place 2 sts on cn and hold at back; K2, K2 from cn

Place 2 sts on cn and hold at front; K2 K2 from cn

Place 1 st on cn and hold at back; K1, K1 from cn
OR K2tog but do not remove from needle, K into
first st then remove both sts tog.

Trinity stitch combined with cables and bobbles

Simple cable patterns separated with rib stitches

Honeycomb worked throughout

Knitting throw pillows is a good way to practice textured stitches.

Skill Level: Easy ◼◼☐☐

One Size: 14" x 14"

MATERIALS

Cables and Rib Pillow: 1 skein of Galway from Plymouth Yarns (100% pure wool; 100 g; 210 yds) in color 142 Lilac (4)

Honeycomb Pillow: 1 skein of Galway Highland Heather from Plymouth Yarns (100% pure wool; 100 g; 210 yds) in color 728 Teal (4)

Trinity Pillow: 1 skein of Galway from Plymouth Yarns (100% pure wool; 100 g; 210 yds) in color 116 Aqua

ALL PILLOWS:

US 8 (5 mm) needles or size required for gauge

Cable needle

Tapestry needle

One 14" x 14" pillow form for each pillow

Optional: 18" x 18" square of cotton fabric (for each pillow) to coordinate with yarn for pillow back

GAUGE

20 sts and 24 rows = 4" in St st patt

Always work a gauge swatch to ensure proper size.

Pattern Note: You can knit two pieces to make the front and back of the pillow, and then sew them together. Or you can use a piece of cotton fabric for the back and sew it to the knitted front.

CABLES AND RIB PILLOW

CO 78 sts. Knit 5 rows.

Work chart A until piece measures approx 12", ending with row 8.

Knit 5 rows. BO all sts.

HONEYCOMB PILLOW

CO 82 sts. Knit 5 rows.

Work chart B until piece measures approx 12", ending with row 2 or row 6.

Knit 5 rows. BO all sts.

TRINITY PILLOW

CO 75 sts and knit 5 rows, inc 3 sts evenly across final row.

Work chart C until piece measures approx 12", ending with row 1 or 15.

Knit 5 rows, dec 3 sts evenly across first row. BO all sts.

Weave in all loose ends. Block gently, being careful not to crush texture.

PILLOW FINISHING

If you knit a piece for the front and the back, sew the two pieces tog using a mattress st, leaving the bottom edge open. Insert a pillow form and use mattress st to close opening.

If you are using fabric for the back, cut fabric to size of knitted front. With RS tog, hand sew the back to the front piece using thread and a sharp needle, or machine sew using a long stitch and being careful not to catch yarn on presser foot. Sew around three sides, leaving bottom edge open. Turn RS out, insert pillow form, and neatly hand sew closed.

Chart A
Cables and rib

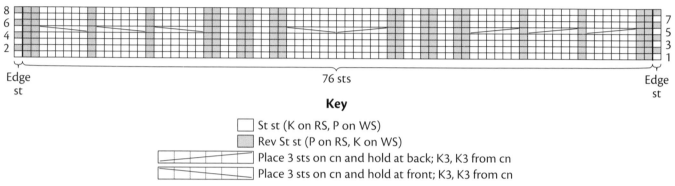

8
6
4
2

7
5
3
1

Edge
st

76 sts

Edge
st

Key

☐ St st (K on RS, P on WS)

▨ Rev St st (P on RS, K on WS)

Place 3 sts on cn and hold at back; K3, K3 from cn

Place 3 sts on cn and hold at front; K3, K3 from cn

Chart B
Honeycomb cable

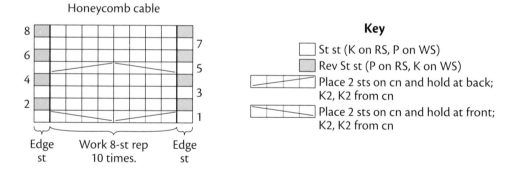

8
6
4
2

7
5
3
1

Edge
st

Work 8-st rep
10 times.

Edge
st

Key

☐ St st (K on RS, P on WS)

▨ Rev St st (P on RS, K on WS)

Place 2 sts on cn and hold at back;
K2, K2 from cn

Place 2 sts on cn and hold at front;
K2, K2 from cn

Chart C
Trinity

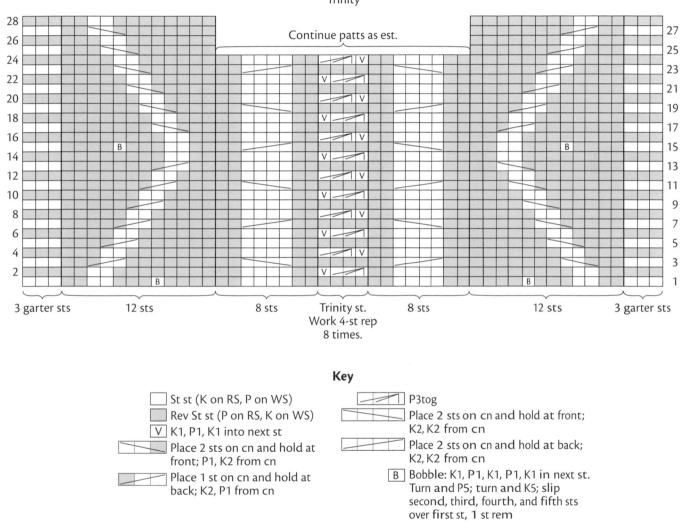

3 garter sts | 12 sts | 8 sts | Trinity st. Work 4-st rep 8 times. | 8 sts | 12 sts | 3 garter sts

Continue patts as est.

Key

	St st (K on RS, P on WS)
	Rev St st (P on RS, K on WS)
V	K1, P1, K1 into next st
	Place 2 sts on cn and hold at front; P1, K2 from cn
	Place 1 st on cn and hold at back; K2, P1 from cn

	P3tog
	Place 2 sts on cn and hold at front; K2, K2 from cn
	Place 2 sts on cn and hold at back; K2, K2 from cn
B	Bobble: K1, P1, K1, P1, K1 in next st. Turn and P5; turn and K5; slip second, third, fourth, and fifth sts over first st, 1 st rem

NELLWYN CARDIGAN

Simple cables offer endless design possibilities;
placing two cables side by side forms the horseshoe cable.

Skill Level: Intermediate ◼◼◼◻

Women's Sizes:
Extra Small (Small, Medium, Large, Extra Large)

Finished Chest: 36 (40, 44, 48, 52)"

Finished Length: 25 (26, 27, 28, 28)"

MATERIALS

9 (11, 12, 13, 14) hanks of Kokopelli from Fiesta Yarns (60% brushed kid mohair, 40% wool; 4 oz; 125 yds) in color K20 Indian Paint Brush

US 8 (5 mm) needles or size required for gauge

US 8 (5 mm) circular needle (32" long) for button band

Seven buttons, size ¾" (20 mm) diameter, (Dill Buttons, style 5-159)

Cable needle

Stitch holders

Tapestry needle

GAUGE

17 sts and 24 rows = 4" in garter st

Ribbing patt (chart A) = 2½" wide

Horseshoe cable (chart D) = 3" wide

Always work a gauge swatch to ensure proper fit.

BACK

CO 72 (76, 83, 94, 102) sts and work in garter st for 1½", inc 40 (42, 41, 36, 34) sts evenly on last WS row—112 (118, 124, 130, 136) sts.

Beg main patt as follows, working row 1 of charts: K1 (edge st), work 3 (6, 9, 12, 15) sts using chart A; work

chart B; *work 9 sts using chart A; work chart D; rep from * twice; work 9 sts using chart A; work chart C; work 3 (6, 9, 12, 15) sts using chart A; K1 (edge st).

Work in est patt until piece measures 24 (25, 26, 27, 27)" from CO edge, ending with WS row.

Neck and shoulders: On next row, work 35 (37, 40, 41, 44) sts in est patt, attach a new ball of yarn and BO center 42 (44, 44, 48, 48) sts, work rem sts.

Work even until piece measures 25 (26, 27, 28, 28)" from CO edge. Place shoulder sts on holders.

RIGHT FRONT

CO 41 (43, 47, 52, 56) sts and work in garter st for 1½". On final WS row, inc 15 (16, 15, 13, 12) sts evenly across row—56 (59, 62, 65, 68) sts.

Beg main patt as follows, working row 1 of charts: K1 (edge st), work chart C; work chart A; work chart D; work chart A; work chart B; work 0 (3, 6, 9, 12) sts using chart A; K1 (edge st).

Work in est patt until piece measures 16 (16½, 17, 18, 17)" from CO edge, ending with WS row.

Neck shaping: K1 (edge st), P1, ssk, work in est patt to end. On next row (WS), work in est patt to last 2 sts, K2. Working in est patt, cont to dec 1 st at neck edge EOR 20 (21, 21, 23, 23) more times—35 (37, 40, 41, 44) sts.

Work even until front measures same as back. Place all sts on holder.

LEFT FRONT

CO 41 (43, 47, 52, 56) sts and work in garter st for 1½". On final WS row, inc 15 (16, 15, 13, 12) sts evenly across row—56 (59, 62, 65, 68) sts.

Beg main patt as follows, working row 1 of charts: K1 (edge st), work 0 (3, 6, 9, 12) sts using chart A; work chart B; work chart A; work chart D; work chart A; work chart C; K1 (edge st).

Work in est patt until piece measures 16 (16½, 17, 18, 17)" from CO edge, ending with RS row.

Neck shaping: Work in est patt to last 4 sts, P2tog, P1, K1 (edge st). On next row (RS), K2, work in est patt across row. Cont to dec 1 st at neck edge EOR 20 (21, 21, 23, 23) more times—35 (37, 40, 41, 44) sts.

Work even until front measures same as back. Place all sts on holder.

SLEEVES ⟨MAKE 2⟩

CO 30 (34, 34, 38, 38) sts and work in garter st for 1½". On final WS row, inc 2 sts—32 (36, 36, 40, 40) sts.

Beg main patt as follows, working row 1 of charts: work 8 (10, 10, 12, 12) sts using chart A; work chart D; work 8 (10, 10, 12, 12) sts using chart A. Inc 1 st at each end on next and every 4 rows for a total of 21 (22, 23, 22, 24) times—74 (80, 82, 84, 88) sts. Work incs in ribbing patt (chart A).

Work even in est patt until piece measures 18 (19, 20, 21, 21)" from CO edge, or desired length. BO all sts in patt.

FINISHING

Seam shoulders using the three-needle bind off (see "Three-Needle Bind Off" at right). Place pins 9 (9½, 10, 10, 11)" from shoulder and sew sleeves between pins. Sew sleeve and side seams.

Neck and Front Bands: Beg at lower right front, PU 69 (73, 77, 80, 80) sts up right front, PU 26 (26, 26, 28, 28) across back, PU 69 (73, 77, 80, 80) down left front—164 (172, 180, 188, 188). Work in garter st for 3 rows. On next row, beg at bottom of right front, work buttonholes as follows: K3 (3, 4, 5, 5) sts, *YO, K2tog; K6 sts; rep from * 5 times; YO, K2tog; knit to end of row. Knit 1 row, then BO loosely. Sew buttons opposite buttonholes.

Weave in all loose ends. Block gently, being careful not to crush texture.

Three-Needle Bind Off

With shoulder stitches on separate needles and right sides tog, use a third needle to knit together one stitch from the front needle and one stitch from the back needle. *Knit together the next stitch on both needles.

Pass the first stitch on the right needle over the second stitch loosely to bind it off. Repeat from * until all stitches are bound off.

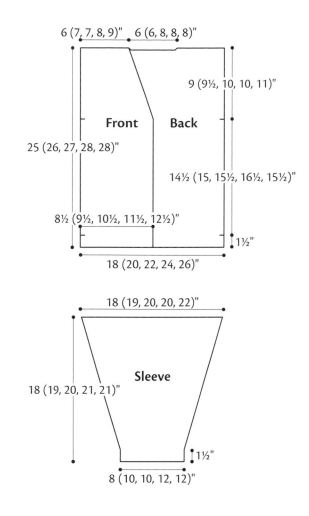

6 (7, 7, 8, 9)"   6 (6, 8, 8, 8)"

9 (9½, 10, 10, 11)"

Front   **Back**

25 (26, 27, 28, 28)"

14½ (15, 15½, 16½, 15½)"

8½ (9½, 10½, 11½, 12½)"

1½"

18 (20, 22, 24, 26)"

18 (19, 20, 20, 22)"

Sleeve

18 (19, 20, 21, 21)"

1½"

8 (10, 10, 12, 12)"

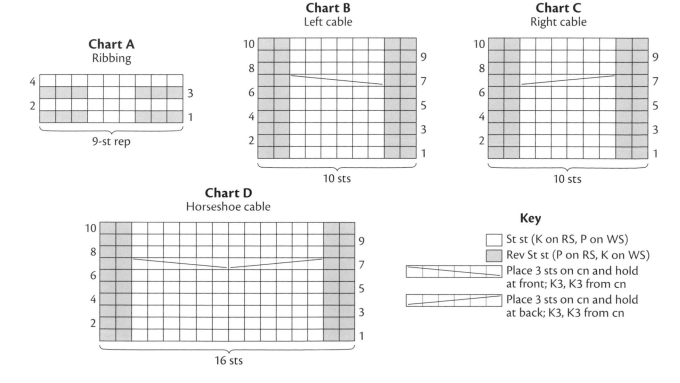

Chart A
Ribbing

9-st rep

Chart B
Left cable

10 sts

Chart C
Right cable

10 sts

Chart D
Horseshoe cable

16 sts

Key

☐ St st (K on RS, P on WS)

▦ Rev St st (P on RS, K on WS)

Place 3 sts on cn and hold at front; K3, K3 from cn

Place 3 sts on cn and hold at back; K3, K3 from cn

FIONA VEST

Allover patterns offer wonderfully interwoven designs.

Skill Level: Intermediate ■■■□

Unisex Sizes: Small (Medium, Large, Extra Large)

Finished Chest: 40 (44, 48, 52)"

Finished Length: 24 (25, 25½, 26)"

MATERIALS

4 (4, 5, 6) hanks of Chuckanut Bay Yarns, distributed by Russi Sales, Inc. (100% Perendale wool; 200 g; 390 yds) in color 297 Beige [4]

US 7 (4.5 mm) needles or size required for gauge

US 7 (4.5 mm) double pointed needles for I-cord trim

20 (22, 22, 24)" separating zipper

Cable needle

Tapestry needle

GAUGE

30 sts and 26 rows = 4" in cable patt

Always work a gauge swatch to ensure proper fit.

BACK

CO 152 (168, 184, 200) sts. Work chart A until piece measures 15", ending with WS row.

Armhole shaping: BO 4 sts at beg of next 2 rows, BO 3 sts at beg of next 4 rows, then dec 1 st each end of needle EOR 8 times—116 (132, 148, 164) sts.

Work even until back measures 8⅞ (9⅞, 10⅜, 10⅞)" from armhole BO, ending with WS row.

Neck shaping: Work in est patt across 38 (38, 46, 52) sts, BO center 40 (56, 56, 60) sts, then work rem sts. Work 1 row even, then BO all sts.

Reattach yarn to other side, work 1 row even, then BO all sts.

RIGHT FRONT

CO 76 (86, 92, 102) sts. Work chart A with the following changes to chart:

For Small: Add 2 rev St sts to beg and end of chart.

For Medium: Delete 1 rev St st at beg and end of chart.

For Large: Add 2 rev St sts to beg and end of chart.

For Extra Large: Delete 1 rev St st at beg and end of chart.

For all sizes: Work chart until piece measures 15", ending with RS row.

Armhole shaping: BO 4 sts at beg of next row, work 1 row even. BO 3 sts EOR twice, then dec 1 st EOR 8 times—58 (68, 74, 84) sts.

Work even until piece measures 6 (7, 7½, 8)" from armhole BO, ending with WS row.

Neck shaping: BO 4 sts at beg of next row, then BO 3 sts at beg of EOR 9 (9, 10, 11) times. Work even on 27 (37, 40, 47) sts until front measures same as back. BO all sts in patt.

LEFT FRONT

Work as for right front until piece measures 15", ending with WS row.

Armhole shaping: BO 4 sts at beg next row, work 1 row even, BO 3 sts EOR twice, then dec 1 st EOR 8 times—58 (68, 74, 84) sts.

Work even until piece measures 6 (7, 7½, 8)" from armhole BO, ending with RS row.

Neck shaping: BO 4 sts at beg of next row; BO 3 sts at beg of EOR 9 (9, 10, 11) times. Work even until same length as back. BO all sts in patt.

FINISHING

Join shoulders with I-cord (see right).

Sew side seams leaving bottom 2" open.

Starting at side seam, trim armholes with attached I-cord. Starting at side seam, trim fronts, neck and bottom edges including side slits with attached I-cord.

Sew zipper in place, adjusting length as necessary. I recommend sewing zipper by hand to give more control while sewing. The textured stitches can easily get caught in the presser foot or the needle of the machine, and if any adjustments need to be made, hand stitches are far easier to remove than machine stitches.

Weave in all loose ends. Block gently, being careful not to crush texture.

Attached I-Cord Trim

For shoulders: Using dpns, CO 3 sts, do not turn work, slide sts to other end of needle. *PU 1 st from back shoulder and work K2tog with first st from I-cord, K1, PU 1 st from front shoulder and work ssk with third st from I-cord. Slide the 3 sts just worked to other end of needle and rep from * until edge is covered. Tug slightly after first st to keep tension even.

For neck, fronts, and bottom edges: Using dpns, CO 3 sts, do not turn work, slide sts to other end of needle. *K2, sl last st from I-cord, PU 1 st from vest and work K2tog with the slipped st. Slide the 3 sts just worked to other end of needle and rep from * until edge is covered. Tug slightly to keep tension even. To make a smooth turn at corners, work into the same st on the vest 3 times.

Weave ends neatly into I-cord, overlapping ends to close any gap.

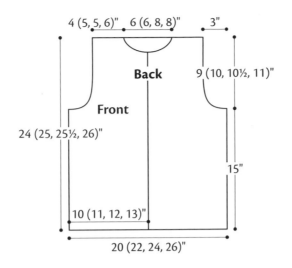

4 (5, 5, 6)"   6 (6, 8, 8)"   3"

Back

9 (10, 10½, 11)"

Front

24 (25, 25½, 26)"

15"

10 (11, 12, 13)"

20 (22, 24, 26)"

Chart A
Fiona (multiple of 16 sts + 8)

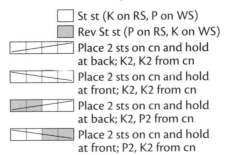

Plus sts

Work 16-st rep 9 (10, 11, 12) times
for back, 4 (5, 5, 6) times for fronts.

Plus sts

Key

☐ St st (K on RS, P on WS)

■ Rev St st (P on RS, K on WS)

Place 2 sts on cn and hold
at back; K2, K2 from cn

Place 2 sts on cn and hold
at front; K2, K2 from cn

Place 2 sts on cn and hold
at back; K2, P2 from cn

Place 2 sts on cn and hold
at front; P2, K2 from cn

SKYLAR FELTED BAG

Fill this bag with all your project needs,
then fold it away when not in use.

Skill Level: Intermediate ◼◼◼◻

One size: Approx 18" wide x 14" long x 6" deep after felting

MATERIALS

12 hanks of Renaissance from Classic Elite Yarns (100% wool; 50 g; 110 yds) in color 7136 Cork 〔4〕

US 9 (5.5 mm) needles or size required for gauge

Cable needle

Tapestry needle

GAUGE

18 sts and 32 rows = 4" in garter st before felting

Always work a gauge swatch to ensure proper size.

Pattern Note: The bag is knit in three pieces, assembled, and then felted. The handles are felted and then sewn so that they may be placed at the desired spot on the felted bag.

If preferred, the handles may certainly be sewn first and then felted into the bag; however, handle placement will be very difficult to change if necessary.

FRONT AND BACK

Make 2 pieces the same.

CO 134 sts and knit 3 rows.

Beg main patt as follows, working row 1 of charts: K2 (edge sts); work charts A, *B, A*; rep from * to * 3 times; K2 (edge sts). Work 30 rows of charts a total of 4 times. Knit 3 rows, then BO all sts in patt.

SIDES AND BOTTOM

Measure down one side of the front piece, across the bottom, and up the other side. CO 25 sts and work in garter st until piece equals this measurement. BO all sts. Sew this piece to front and back pieces.

HANDLES 〈MAKE 2〉

CO 7 sts and work in garter st until handle measures approx 16" or desired length. BO all sts. Note that after felting the handle will stretch a bit when the bag is carried.

FINISHING

Weave in all loose ends. Place bag and handles into washing machine and run through one cycle with hot water and a small amount of detergent. Remove and shape bag over cardboard boxes; pin handles to a flat surface. When completely dry, sew ends of handles approx 10" apart, centered on front and back of bag.

Cables, due to their interesting raised elements, are wonderful even when felted.

Chart A

Chart B

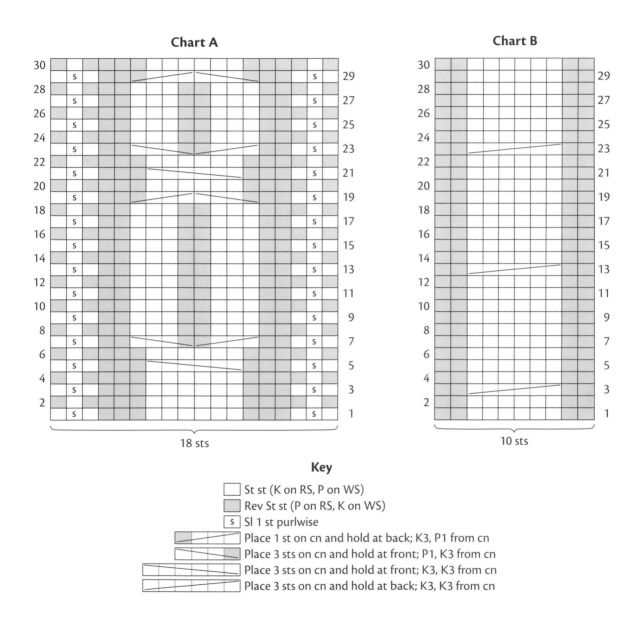

Key

☐	St st (K on RS, P on WS)
▨	Rev St st (P on RS, K on WS)
s	Sl 1 st purlwise
	Place 1 st on cn and hold at back; K3, P1 from cn
	Place 3 sts on cn and hold at front; P1, K3 from cn
	Place 3 sts on cn and hold at front; K3, K3 from cn
	Place 3 sts on cn and hold at back; K3, K3 from cn

ROBIN PULLOVER AND TAM

Everyone loves the OXO and honeycomb stitch patterns,
both of which utilize two knit stitches crossing over two knit stitches.
The Robin Pullover is a wonderful design for a mother/daughter duo.
Extra Small will fit girls age 6–8, and Small will fit girls age 10–12.

Skill Level: Intermediate ■■■▭

Girls' and Women's Sweater Sizes:
Extra Small (Small, Medium,
Large, Extra Large)

Finished Sweater Chest:
30 (36, 40, 44, 48)"

Finished Sweater Length:
18 (20, 23, 24, 26)"

Tam Circumference: 18 (20, 22)"

MATERIALS

Waterlily from Classic Elite Yarns
(100% extra fine merino; 50 g; 100
yds) in color 1988 Goldfish ⑷

14 (19, 24, 28, 32) balls for sweater

2 (2, 2) balls for tam

US 8 (5 mm) needles or size required
for gauge

US 7 (4.5 mm) circular needle
(24" long) for tam and neckband

US 7 (4.5 mm) double pointed needles
for tam

US 6 (4.25 mm) circular needle for tam

Cable needle

Stitch markers

Stitch holder

Tapestry needle

GAUGE

20 sts and 24 rows = 4" in moss st patt
on largest needles

OXO cable and honeycomb cable
= 1½" wide x 2½" high on largest
needles

Always work a gauge swatch to
ensure proper fit.

SWEATER BACK

CO 82 (100, 112, 116, 128) sts and
set up ribbing patt as follows:

For Extra Small: K1 (edge st); K1, (P1,
K1) 6 times; P1, K2, P2, K2, P1; (K1,
P1) 5 times; K2, (P2, K2) 4 times; (P1,
K1) 5 times; P1, K2, P2, K2, P1; K1,
(P1, K1) 6 times; K1 (edge st).

For Small: K1 (edge st); (P1, K1) 9
times; P1, K2, P2, K2, P1; (K1, P1) 5
times; K2, (P2, K2) 6 times; (P1, K1) 5
times; P1, K2, P2, K2, P1; (K1, P1) 9
times; K1 (edge st).

For Medium: K1 (edge st); (P1, K1) 9
times; P1, K2, P2, K2, P1; (K1, P1) 5
times; K2, (P2, K2) 9 times; (P1, K1) 5
times; P1, K2, P2, K2, P1; (K1, P1) 9
times; K1 (edge st).

For Large: K1 (edge st); (P1, K1) 9
times; P1, K2, P2, K2, P1; (K1, P1) 5
times; K2, (P2, K2) 10 times; (P1, K1)
5 times; P1, K2, P2, K2, P1; (K1, P1)
9 times; K1 (edge st).

For Extra Large: K1 (edge st); (P1, K1)
10 times; P1, K2, P2, K2, P1; (K1, P1)
5 times; K2, (P2, K2) 12 times; (P1,
K1) 5 times; P1, K2, P2, K2, P1; (K1,
P1) 10 times; K1 (edge st).

For all sizes: Work ribbing for 2",
ending with WS row.

Beg main patt as follows, working
row 1 of charts, and making incs on
first row only: K1 (edge st), work 4 (9,
9, 9, 11) sts using chart A; work chart

B; work chart C with incs as P1, K2, M1, K2, M1, K2, P1; work chart B; work 1 st in rev St st; pm; work chart D 3 (4, 6, 7, 8) times while inc 6 (6, 10, 14, 14) sts evenly; pm; work 1 st in rev St st; work chart B; work chart C with incs as P1, K2, M1, K2, M1, K2, P1; work chart B; work 4 (9, 9, 9, 11) sts using chart A, K1 (edge st)—92 (110, 126, 134, 146) sts.

Work in est patt until piece measures 18 (20, 23, 24, 26)" from CO edge. BO all sts in patt; dec honeycomb and OXO cables if necessary to avoid cable flare.

SWEATER FRONT

Work as for back until piece measures 15 (17, 20, 21, 23)" from CO edge, ending with WS row.

Neck shaping: Work 39 (47, 53, 56, 62) sts, attach a new ball of yarn and BO center 14 (16, 20, 22, 22) sts, work rem sts. At each neck edge BO 3 sts 1 (1, 2, 2, 3) times; BO 2 sts 2 (3, 2, 3, 2) times; dec 1 st EOR 3 (2, 3, 2, 1) times—29 (36, 40, 42, 48) sts for each shoulder.

Work even until piece measures same as back. BO all sts in patt; dec honeycomb and OXO cables if necessary to avoid cable flare.

SLEEVES ‹MAKE 2›

CO 39 (39, 39, 43, 47) sts. Est ribbing as follows: K1 (edge st), (P1, K1) 3 (3, 3, 4, 5) times, P1; K2, P2, K2; P1; (K1, P1) 5 times; K2, P2, K2; P1, (K1, P1) 3 (3, 3, 4, 5) times; K1 (edge st). Work for 2", ending with WS row.

Beg main patt as follows, working row 1 of charts and making incs on first row only: K1 (edge st), work 6 (6, 6, 8, 10) sts using chart A; work chart C with incs as P1, K2, M1, K2, M1, K2, P1; work chart B; work chart C with inc as P1, K2, M1, K2, M1, K2, P1; work 6 (6, 6, 8, 10) sts using chart A, K1 (edge st)—43 (43, 43, 47, 51) sts.

Work in est patt and AT THE SAME TIME inc 1 st each end of row every 4 (4, 3, 3, 3) rows 19 (23, 33, 36, 39) times—81 (89, 109, 119, 129) sts.

Work even until sleeve measures 14 (16, 18, 19, 20)" from CO edge, or desired length, ending with WS row.

Saddle: On next row, BO 35 (39, 49, 54, 59) sts; work 1 st in rev St st; cont chart B; work 1 st in rev St st; work rem sts. On next row, BO 35 (39, 49, 54, 59) sts. Work 11 sts as est until saddle measures approx 5 (6, 7, 7½, 8)" and place all sts on holder.

SWEATER FINISHING

Sew saddle sections between back and front pieces, adjusting length as necessary. Place pins 6 (7, 8, 9, 10)" down from midpoint of saddle and sew sleeves between these pins. Sew sleeve and side seams.

Neckband: Using circular needle, beg at back right, PU 31 (39, 45, 53, 53) sts around neck; K11 from holder; PU 39 (47, 53, 61, 61) sts around front neck; K11 from holder—92 (108, 120, 136, 136) sts. Pm, join into rnd and work K2, P2 ribbing around neck for 5 (6, 6, 7, 7)" or desired length. BO all sts in patt.

Weave in all loose ends. Block gently, being careful not to crush texture or distort ribbing.

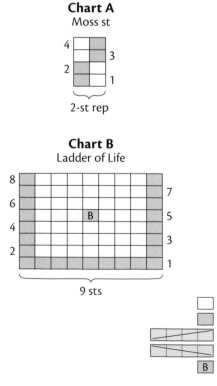

Chart A
Moss st

2-st rep

Chart B
Ladder of Life

9 sts

Chart C
OXO cable

10 sts

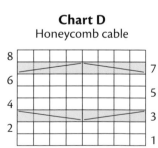

Chart D
Honeycomb cable

8-st rep

Key

□ St st (K on RS, P on WS)
▨ Rev St st (P on RS, K on WS)
▱ Place 2 sts on cn and hold at back; K2, K2 from cn
▱ Place 2 sts on cn and hold at front; K2, K2 from cn
B Bobble: K1, P1, K1, P1, K1 in next st. Turn and K5; turn and P5; slip second, third, fourth, and fifth sts over first st, 1 st rem

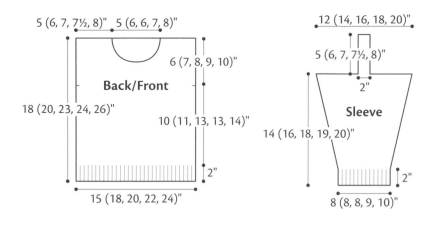

5 (6, 7, 7½, 8)" 5 (6, 6, 7, 8)"

12 (14, 16, 18, 20)"

6 (7, 8, 9, 10)"

Back/Front

18 (20, 23, 24, 26)"

10 (11, 13, 13, 14)"

2"

15 (18, 20, 22, 24)"

5 (6, 7, 7½, 8)"

2"

Sleeve

14 (16, 18, 19, 20)"

2"

8 (8, 8, 9, 10)"

ROBIN TAM

Using smaller circular needle, CO 90 (100, 110) sts, pm, join and work in K1, P1 ribbing for 6 (8, 10) rnds. Change to St st and work 2 rnds. On next rnd, *inc 10 sts evenly around. Work 2 (4, 4) rnds even. Rep from * twice more—120 (130, 140) sts. Next rnd, purl for turning rnd.

Switch to larger circular needle. Beg main patt as follows and work row 1 of charts: *work chart C; work 14 (16, 18) sts in chart A; rep from * 4 times. Work in est patt reading charts from right to left. AT THE SAME TIME dec 1 st at each end of moss st sections on following rnds:

Rnd 6—110 (120, 130) sts.

Rnd 8—100 (110, 120) sts.

Rnd 10—90 (100, 110) sts.

Rnd 12—80 (90, 100) sts.

Rnd 14—70 (80, 90) sts.

Rnd 16—60 (70, 80) sts.

On Medium and Large: Dec 1 st at each end of moss st sections on rnd 18—(60, 70) sts.

On Large: Dec 1 st at each end of moss st sections on rnd 20—60 sts.

Change to dpns when pattern becomes difficult to work.

Rnd 17 (19, 21): P2tog on rem moss sts—55 sts.

Rnd 18 and 19 (rnd 20 and 21, rnd 22 and 23): Work even; purl rem moss st.

Rnd 20 (22, 24): Dec purl sts by working P3tog with first and last st of OXO cable—45 sts.

Rnd 21 (23, 25): *P1, K6, ssk; rep from * 4 times—40 sts.

Rnd 22 (24, 26): *K2tog, K4, ssk; rep from * 4 times—30 sts.

Rnd 23 (25, 27): *K2tog, K2, ssk; rep from * 4 times—20 sts.

Rnd 24 (26, 28): *K2tog, ssk; rep from * 4 times—10 sts.

Rnd 25 (27, 29): K2tog 5 times—5 sts.

Cut yarn leaving a tail, then using tapestry needle, thread needle through rem sts and tighten to close hole.

Block tam by using a small dinner plate to shape. Place edge of plate at turning rnd and pin down to a padded surface.

Optional: Make 1 thick pom-pom, then attach to top of tam using the tail from the knitting.

Emer Pullover

The classic Aran diamond filled with seed stitch
is taken a step further by connecting it with cables.

Skill Level: Intermediate ◼◼◼◻

Women's Sizes: Small (Medium, Large, Extra Large)

Finished Chest: 40 (44, 48, 52)"

Finished Length: 24 (25, 26, 27)"

MATERIALS

4 (5, 5, 6) hanks of Chuckanut Bay Yarns distributed by Russi Sales, Inc. (100% Perendale wool; 200 g; 390 yds) in color 304 Ocean Blue ④

US 8 (5 mm) needles or size required for gauge

US 8 (5 mm) circular needle (32" long) for neckband

Cable needle

Stitch holders

Tapestry needle

GAUGE

20 sts and 21 rows = 4" in rev St st

Diamond motif over 21 sts (chart A) = 3½" wide

Braid patt over 20 sts (chart B) = 3½" wide

Always work a gauge swatch to ensure proper fit.

Pattern Note: When binding off cables A and B, work 2 sts together 3 times (beginning of cable, middle of cable and end of cable) to keep cables in proper proportion.

BACK

CO 101 (111, 121, 133) sts. Work in K1, P1 ribbing for 1", inc 10 (12, 14, 14) sts evenly on last WS row—111 (123, 135, 147) sts.

Beg main patt, working row 1 of charts: K1 (edge st); work chart D 2 (3, 4, 5) times; work 2 sts in rev St st; work charts in order as follows: C, B, C, A, C, B, C; work 2 sts in rev St st; work chart D 2 (3, 4, 5) times; K1 (edge st).

Work in est patt until piece measures 16 (16, 16½, 17)" from CO edge, ending with WS row.

Armhole shaping: BO 3 sts at beg of next 2 rows, then dec 1 st at each end EOR 5 (6, 7, 8) times—95 (105, 115, 125) sts.

Work even in est patt until back measures 23½ (24½, 25½, 26½)", ending with WS row.

Neck shaping: Work 29 (34, 36, 39) sts in est patt, attach a new ball of yarn and BO center 37 (37, 43, 47) sts, work rem sts. Work 1 row even, then dec 1 st at each neck edge EOR 2 times—27 (32, 34, 37) sts for each shoulder.

Work even in est patt until back measures 24 (25, 26, 27)". BO all sts in patt.

FRONT

Work as for back until piece measures 21 (22, 23, 24)" from CO edge, ending with WS row.

Neck shaping: Work 32 (37, 39, 42) sts in est patt, attach a new ball of yarn and BO center 31 (31, 37, 41) sts, work rem sts in patt. BO 2 sts at each neck edge; dec 1 st each neck edge 3 times—27 (32, 34, 37) sts for each shoulder.

Work even in est patt until front measures same as back. BO all sts in patt.

SLEEVES ⟨MAKE 2⟩

CO 44 (44, 54, 54) sts. Work in K1, P1 ribbing for 1", inc 4 (4, 6, 6) sts evenly on last WS row—48 (48, 60, 60) sts.

Beg main patt as follows: K1 (edge st); work chart D 1 (1, 2, 2) times; work 2 sts in rev St st; work charts C, B, C; work 2 sts in rev St st; work chart D 1 (1, 2, 2) times; K1 (edge st). AT THE SAME TIME inc 1 st each end every 3 rows 5 (20, 5, 15) times, then every 4

rows 19 (10, 23, 16) times—96 (108, 116, 122) sts. Work incs into chart D.

Work even until sleeve edge measures 16 (17, 18, 19)" from CO edge, or desired length, ending with RS row.

Cap shaping: BO 3 sts at beg of next 2 rows, then dec 1 st at each end EOR 5 (6, 7, 8) times—80 (90, 96, 100) sts. It is easiest to work decs on WS rows as follows: K1 (edge st), P2tog, work to last 3 sts, P2tog tbl, K1 (edge st).

Work 1 row even, then BO all sts in patt.

FINISHING

Sew shoulder seams, matching cable patterns. Pin sleeves in armhole area and sew. Sew sleeve and side seams.

Neckband: Using circular needle, PU 84 (90, 94, 100) sts evenly around neck, pm and join into rnd. Work K1, P1 ribbing for 1" or desired length. BO all sts in patt.

Weave in all loose ends. Block gently, being careful not to crush texture or distort ribbing.

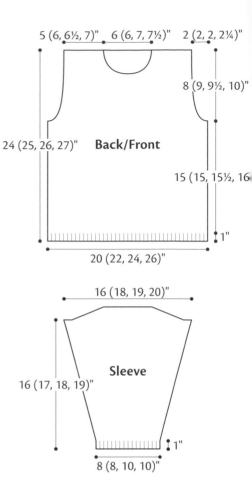

5 (6, 6½, 7)"   6 (6, 7, 7½)"   2 (2, 2, 2¼)"

8 (9, 9½, 10)"

24 (25, 26, 27)"   **Back/Front**

15 (15, 15½, 16)"

1"

20 (22, 24, 26)"

16 (18, 19, 20)"

16 (17, 18, 19)"   **Sleeve**

1"

8 (8, 10, 10)"

Chart A

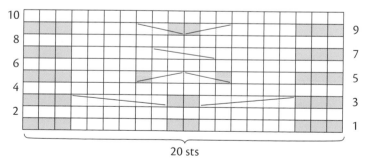

36
34
32
30
28
26
24
22
20
18
16
14
12
10
8
6
4
2

35
33
31
29
27
25
23
21
19
17
15
13
11
9
7
5
3
1

21 sts

Key

☐ St st (K on RS, P on WS)

▨ Rev St st (P on RS, K on WS)

Place 1 st on cn and hold at back; K2, K1 from cn

Place 2 sts on cn and hold at front; K1, K2 from cn

Place 2 sts on cn and hold at back; K2, K2 from cn

Place 2 sts on cn and hold at front; K2, K2 from cn

Place 4 sts on cn and hold at back; K2, K4 from cn

Place 2 sts on cn and hold at front; K4, K2 from cn

Place 2 sts on cn and hold at front; P1, K2 from cn

Place 1 st on cn and hold at back; K2, P1 from cn

Place 1 st on cn and hold at back; K1, K1 from cn

Place 1 st on cn and hold at front; K1, K1 from cn

Chart B

10
8
6
4
2

9
7
5
3
1

20 sts

Chart C

4
2

3
1

5 sts

Chart D

8
6
4
2

7
5
3
1

6-st rep

SINEAD PULLOVER

*An excellent, all-purpose textured sweater
suitable for men as well as women.*

Skill Level: Intermediate ■■■□

Unisex Sizes: Small (Medium, Large, Extra Large)

Finished Chest: 40 (44, 48, 52)"

Finished Length: 24 (26, 27, 28)"

MATERIALS

13 (15, 17, 19) hanks of Renaissance from Classic Elite Yarns (100% wool; 50 g; 110 yds) in color 7118 Basil 🌀4

US 8 (5 mm) needles or size required for gauge

US 8 (5 mm) circular needle (32" long) for neckband

Cable needle

Tapestry needle

GAUGE

19 sts and 24 rows = 4" in St st

Chart A (measured over 22 sts) = 3.25" wide

Chart B (measured over 22 sts) = 3" wide

Always work a gauge swatch to ensure proper fit.

BACK

CO 136 (148, 160, 172) sts and work in K2, P2 ribbing for 1", ending with WS row.

Beg main patt as follows, working row 1 of charts: K1 (edge st); work 0 (6, 6, 12) sts in rev St st; work chart C 0 (0, 1, 1) times; work charts in order as follows: B, C, A, C, B, C, A, C, B; work chart C 0 (0, 1, 1) times; work 0 (6, 6, 12) sts in rev St st; K1 (edge st).

Work in est patt until piece measures 23½ (25½, 26½, 27½)" from CO edge, ending with WS row.

Neck shaping: Work 50 (54, 58, 61) sts in est patt; attach a new ball of yarn and BO center 36 (40, 44, 50) sts, work rem sts. BO 2 sts at each neck edge once—48 (52, 56, 59) sts for each shoulder.

Work 1 row even. BO all sts in patt.

FRONT

Work as for back until piece measures 20 (22, 23, 24)", ending with WS row.

Neck shaping: Work 56 (60, 66, 69) sts in est patt; attach a new ball of yarn and BO center 24 (28, 28, 34) sts; work rem sts. At each neck edge, BO 3 sts once, BO 2 sts twice, then dec 1 st 1 (1, 3, 3) time—48 (52, 56, 59) sts on each shoulder.

Work even in est patt until piece measures same as back. BO all sts in patt.

FINISHING

Sew shoulders tog, matching cable patterns. Place pins 9 (10, 10, 11)" from top of shoulder and sew sleeves between pins. Sew sleeve and side seams.

Neckband: PU 92 (100, 104, 112) sts evenly around neck. Pm, join and work in K2, P2 ribbing until neckband measures 1½", or desired length. BO all sts in patt.

Weave in all loose ends. Block gently, being careful not to crush texture or distort ribbing.

The classic cable is bordered by traveling stitches to give it an added dimension.

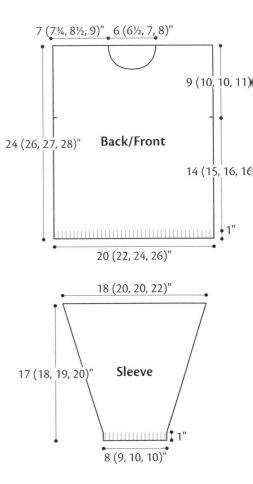

SLEEVES ⟨MAKE 2⟩

CO 46 (50, 54, 58) sts and work in K2, P2 ribbing for 1", ending with WS row.

Beg main patt as follows, working row 1 of charts: work 6 (8, 10, 12) sts as indicated for beg sleeve on chart A; work charts C, A, C; work 6 (8, 10, 12) sts as indicated for end of sleeve on chart A.

Work in est patt, inc 1 st each end on next and every 3 rows for a total of 33 (35, 33, 35) times—112 (120, 120, 128) sts. Incs should complete patt A, then patt C. When you have 90 sts on needle, consisting of patts C, A, C, A, C, A, C, work rem 11 (15, 15, 19) inc sts on each side in rev St st.

Work even in est patt until sleeve measures 17 (18, 19, 20)" from CO edge, or desired length. BO all sts in patt.

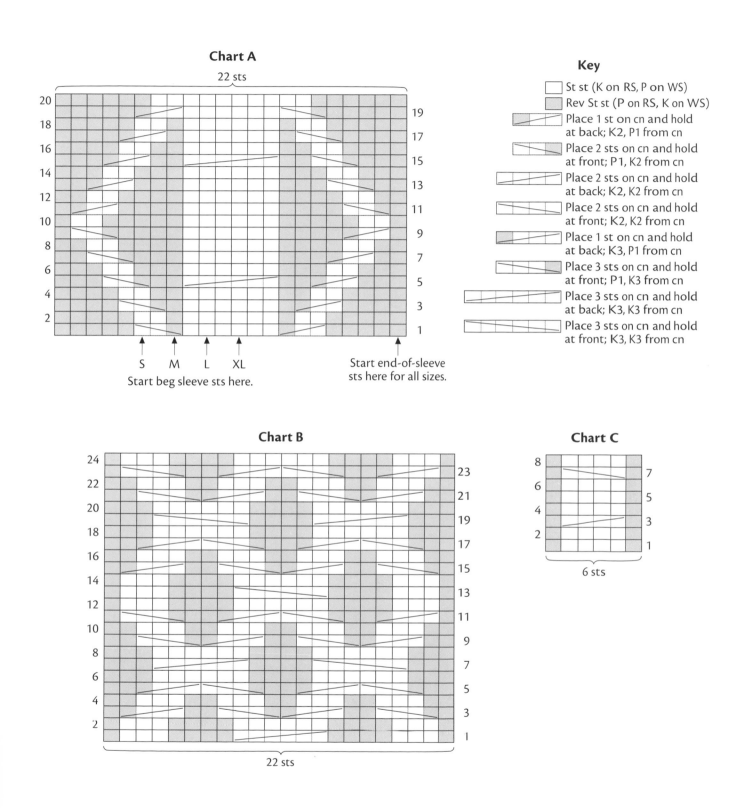

Chart A

22 sts

S   M   L   XL

Start beg sleeve sts here.

Start end-of-sleeve
sts here for all sizes.

Key

☐ St st (K on RS, P on WS)

▨ Rev St st (P on RS, K on WS)

Place 1 st on cn and hold
at back; K2, P1 from cn

Place 2 sts on cn and hold
at front; P1, K2 from cn

Place 2 sts on cn and hold
at back; K2, K2 from cn

Place 2 sts on cn and hold
at front; K2, K2 from cn

Place 1 st on cn and hold
at back; K3, P1 from cn

Place 3 sts on cn and hold
at front; P1, K3 from cn

Place 3 sts on cn and hold
at back; K3, K3 from cn

Place 3 sts on cn and hold
at front; K3, K3 from cn

Chart B

22 sts

Chart C

6 sts

LUCY V-NECK PULLOVER

This lovely sweater is another design utilizing the honeycomb cable, the OXO cable, and a simple cable.

Skill Level: Intermediate ◼◼◼◻

Teen and Women's Sizes: Extra Small (Small, Medium, Large, Extra Large)

Finished Bust: 32 (36, 40, 44, 48)"

Finished Length: 21 (23, 24, 25, 26)"

MATERIALS

7 (9, 10, 11, 13) hanks of Montera from Classic Elite Yarns (50% llama, 50% wool; 100 g; 127 yds) in color 3826 Andes Lavender ⑤

US 8 (5 mm) needles or size required for gauge

US 7 (4.5 mm) circular needle (32" long) for V-neck collar

Cable needle

Tapestry needle

GAUGE

16 sts and 24 rows = 4" in St st on larger needles

Honeycomb cable over 24 sts (chart C) = 4" wide

Always work a gauge swatch to ensure proper fit.

BACK

With larger needles, CO 96 (100, 104, 112, 116) sts and set up ribbing as follows:

Extra Small: K1 (edge st); K2, P2; work chart D; P4, K2, P2, K2, P4; work chart D; P2, (K2, P2) 12 times; work chart D; P4, K2, P2, K2, P4; work chart D; P2, K2; K1 (edge st).

Small: K1 (edge st), P2, K2, P2; work chart D; P4, K2, P2, K2, P4; work chart D; P2, (K2, P2) 12 times; work chart D; P4, K2, P2, K2, P4; work chart D; P2, K2, P2; K1 (edge st).

Medium: K1 (edge st), (K2, P2) twice; work chart D; P4, K2, P2, K2, P4; work chart D; P2, (K2, P2) 12 times; work chart D; P4, K2, P2, K2, P4; work chart D; (P2, K2) twice; K1 (edge st).

Large: K1 (edge st); (K2, P2) twice; work chart D; P4, K2, P2, K2, P4; work chart D; P2, (K2, P2) 14 times; work chart D; P4, K2, P2, K2, P4; work chart D; (P2, K2) twice; K1 (edge st).

Extra Large: K1 (edge st), P2, (K2, P2) twice; work chart D; P4, K2, P2, K2, P4; work chart D; P2, (K2, P2) 14 times; work chart D; P4, K2, P2, K2, P4; work chart D; P2, (K2, P2) twice; K1 (edge st).

For all sizes: Work in est ribbing for 1½", ending with WS row.

Beg main patt as follows, working row 1 of charts, and making incs in first row only: K1 (edge st); work 2 (4, 6, 6, 8) sts in St st; work 2 sts in rev St st; work chart A; work chart B with inc as P2, K1, M1, K4, M1, K1, P2; work chart C 4 (4, 4, 5, 5) times while inc 1 st at each end on first row; work chart B with inc as P2, K1, M1, K4, M1, K1, P2; work chart A; work 2 sts in rev St st; work 2 (4, 6, 6, 8) sts in St st; K1 (edge st)—102 (106, 110, 118, 122) sts.

Work in est patt until piece measures 20½ (22½, 23½, 24½, 25½)", ending with WS row.

Neck shaping: Work 31 (33, 35, 37, 39) sts, attach a new ball of yarn and BO center 40 (40, 40, 44, 44) sts; work rem sts. BO 2 sts at neck edge on next 2 rows—29 (31, 33, 35, 37) sts for each shoulder.

Work even in est patt until piece measures 21 (23, 24, 25, 26)" from CO edge. BO all sts in patt.

FRONT

Work as for back until piece measures 13 (14½, 15½, 16, 16½)" from CO edge, ending with WS row.

Neck shaping: Work in est patt across 51 (53, 55, 59, 61) sts, attach a new ball of yarn and work rem sts with new yarn. Work 1 row even. On next and all RS rows, work to last 3 sts before V-neck separation, K2tog, K1. After V-neck separation K1, ssk, and work across row. Cont dec until you have 29 (31, 33, 35, 37) sts on each shoulder.

Work even in est patt until piece measures same as back. BO all sts in patt.

SLEEVES ⟨MAKE 2⟩

CO 46 sts. Set up ribbing as follows: K1 (edge st); P4, K2, P2, K2, P4; work chart D; P2, K3, P2, K3, P2; work chart D; P4, K2, P2, K2, P4; K1 (edge st). On WS rows, knit the knit sts and purl the purl sts as they face you. Work in est patt until ribbing measures 1½".

Beg main patt as follows, working row 1 of charts: K1 (edge st); work 4 sts in rev St st; work 6-st cable from chart A; work 4 sts in rev St st; work chart D; work chart B; work chart D; work 4 sts in rev St st; work 6-st cable from chart A; work 4 sts in rev St st; K1 (edge st).

Work in est patt and AT THE SAME TIME inc 1 st each end on next and every 5 (5, 5, 4, 4) rows, working incs

as follows: 1 st in rev St st, chart D, then all rem incs in rev St st. Work incs until sleeve length measures 16 (17, 18, 19, 20)" from CO edge. BO all sts in patt.

FINISHING

Sew shoulders tog. Place pins 8 (8½, 8½, 9, 9½)" from shoulder seam and sew sleeves between pins. Sew sleeve and side seams.

Neck edging: Leaving a 10" tail for seaming, and beg at V-neck separation, PU 114 (118, 118, 122, 126) sts evenly around neckline. K1 (edge st), then work in K2, P2 ribbing, K1 (edge st). Work back and forth in rows until ribbing measures 1" or desired length. BO all sts in patt. Cross the rib sections at V-neck separation and seam with yarn ends.

Weave in all loose ends. Block gently, being careful not to crush texture or distort ribbing.

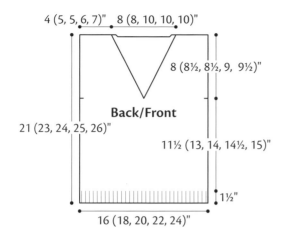

4 (5, 5, 6, 7)"   8 (8, 10, 10, 10)"

8 (8½, 8½, 9, 9½)"

Back/Front

21 (23, 24, 25, 26)"

11½ (13, 14, 14½, 15)"

1½"

16 (18, 20, 22, 24)"

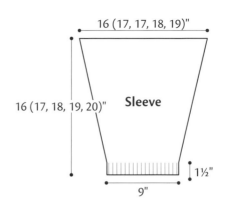

16 (17, 17, 18, 19)"

Sleeve

16 (17, 18, 19, 20)"

1½"

9"

Chart A
18 sts

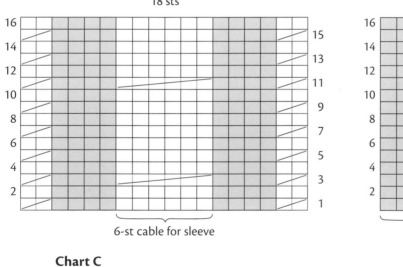

6-st cable for sleeve

Chart B
OXO cable

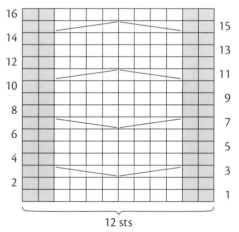

12 sts

Chart C
Honeycomb cable

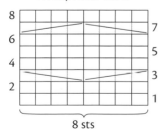

8 sts

Chart D
Mock cable

2 sts

Key

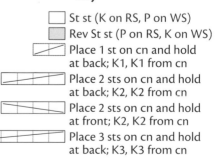

☐ St st (K on RS, P on WS)
▨ Rev St st (P on RS, K on WS)
Place 1 st on cn and hold at back; K1, K1 from cn
Place 2 sts on cn and hold at back; K2, K2 from cn
Place 2 sts on cn and hold at front; K2, K2 from cn
Place 3 sts on cn and hold at back; K3, K3 from cn

CIARAN PULLOVER

Containing simple cables, horseshoe cables, and moss stitches, this pullover looks more complex than it is.

Skill Level: Experienced ▰▰▰▱

Unisex Sizes: Small (Medium, Large, Extra Large)

Finished Chest: 40 (44, 48, 54)"

Finished Length: 28 (28½, 29, 29½)"

MATERIALS

4 (5, 5, 6) hanks of Chuckanut Bay Yarns distributed by Russi Sales, Inc. (100% Perendale wool; 200 g; 390 yds) in color 311 Ginger 🧶4

US 8 (5 mm) needles or size required for gauge

US 8 (5 mm) circular needle (24" long) for neckband

Waste yarn (mercerized cotton is best but not essential) in a contrasting color

Cable needle

Stitch holders

Tapestry needle

GAUGE

20 sts and 25 rows = 4" in St st

19 sts and 25 rows = 4" in moss st patt

Always work a gauge swatch to ensure proper fit.

Pattern Notes: Cable B is shown as a right-crossing cable; this is best worked as a mirrored cable. On right side of work cross to the right, and on left side of work cross to the left. This step is optional.

The lower border is picked up from a provisional cast on and knit downward on a circular needle after the sweater has been completed.

BACK

CO 124 (132, 144, 160) sts using provisional CO technique (see page 72). Set up cable patt as follows:

For Small and Medium: Work 5 (9) sts using chart C; work charts A, B, A over 24 sts; work chart D over 66 sts; work charts A, B, A over 24 sts; work 5 (9) sts using chart C.

For Large: Work 11 sts using chart C; work charts B, A, B, A over 28 sts; work chart D over 66 sts; work charts A, B, A, B over 28 sts; work 11 sts using chart C.

For Extra Large: Work 9 sts using chart C; work charts A, B, A, B, A over 38 sts; work chart D over 66 sts; work charts A, B, A, B, A over 38 sts; work 9 sts using chart C.

For all sizes: Work in est patt for 144 rows (3 reps of chart D). BO all sts, working a K2tog twice within all cable chart A areas.

FRONT

Work as for back for 132 rows.

Neck shaping: Work 50 (54, 56, 60) sts in est patt, attach a new ball of yarn and BO center 24 (24, 32, 40) sts, work rem sts in patt. At each neck edge, BO 3 sts EOR twice, then BO 2 sts EOR twice—40 (44, 46, 50) sts for each shoulder.

Work in est patt to final row of chart, then BO all sts in patt, working a K2tog twice within all chart A cable areas.

SLEEVES (MAKE 2)

CO 48 (48, 56, 56) sts (provisional CO not needed).

Beg main patt as follows, working row 1 of charts: K1 (edge st); S and M only: work LC from chart A; L and XL only: work RC and LC from chart A; for all sizes: work 7 sts using chart C; work charts A, B, A over 24 sts; work 7 sts using chart C; S and M only: work RC from chart A; L and XL only: work RC and LC from chart A; K1 (edge st). Work in est patt, AT THE SAME TIME inc 1 st each end every 4 (4, 3, 3) rows 23 (28, 33, 38) times—94 (104, 122, 132) sts. Work incs into charts A, B, A, then work rem sts in chart C.

Saddle: When sleeve measures 17 (18, 19, 20)" from CO edge, BO 43 (48, 57, 62) sts in patt, working K2tog within chart A cables; work to end of row. On next row, BO 43 (48, 57, 62) sts—8 sts. Work 2 sts in rev St st; work chart B, work 2 sts in rev St st. Cont in est patt on 8 sts until saddle measures approx 6½ (7½, 8, 8½)", place sts on holder.

FINISHING

Sew saddle sections between back and front shoulders adjusting length as necessary. Place pins 8 (9, 9½, 10)" from midpoint of saddle and sew sleeves between pins. Sew sleeve and side seams.

Neckband: Starting at left shoulder, K8 from holder; PU 52 (54, 56, 58) sts across front; K8 from holder; PU 46 (48, 50, 52) sts across back—114 (118, 122, 126 sts). Pm, join into rnd and work in K1b, P1 ribbing for 1" or desired length. BO all sts in patt.

Lower border: Very carefully put sts from provisional CO onto circular needle. There should be 248 (264, 288, 320) sts on the needle. Join, pm and working circularly, purl 1 round; dec 20 sts from bulky or flaring areas by working K2tog in cables until there are 228 (244, 268, 300) sts on needle. Knit 1 rnd, purl 1 rnd, and then work in St st (knit every rnd) until St st section measures 5 (5½, 6, 6½)" or desired length. Work in K1b, P1 ribbing for 1". BO all stitches in patt.

Weave in all loose ends. Block gently, being careful not to crush texture or distort ribbing.

Provisional Cast On

A provisional cast on is temporary, and will be removed later so that the live stitches remain intact.

1. Use a crochet hook and make a number of loose chain stitches with a contrasting slippery yarn, such as a mercerized cotton. Make one chain for each stitch of cast on plus a few extra.

2. Using a knitting needle, knit into the back of each chain with the yarn that will be used in the pattern. Begin knitting as instructed in the pattern.

Knit into the back of each chain.

3. To pick up the stitches, remove the crochet chain by pulling each chain out one at a time and placing the live stitches back on the knitting needle.

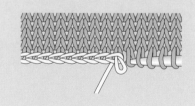

Simple cables and double cables lead the eye out toward the edge pattern.

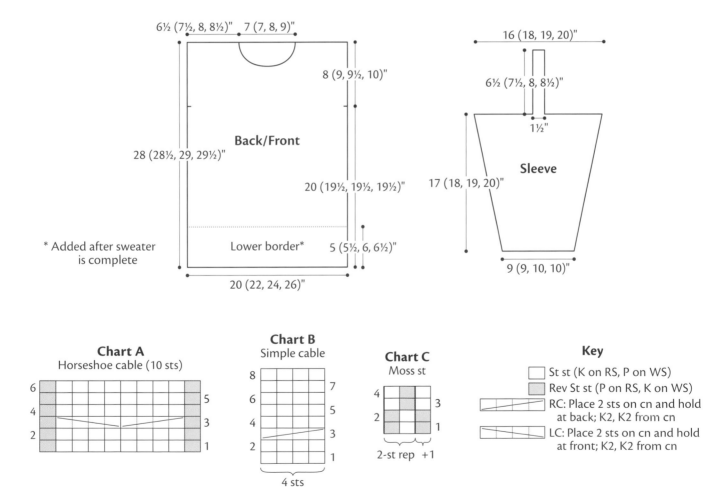

6½ (7½, 8, 8½)"   7 (7, 8, 9)"

8 (9, 9½, 10)"

Back/Front

28 (28½, 29, 29½)"

20 (19½, 19½, 19½)"

* Added after sweater
is complete

Lower border*   5 (5½, 6, 6½)"

20 (22, 24, 26)"

16 (18, 19, 20)"

6½ (7½, 8, 8½)"

1½"

Sleeve

17 (18, 19, 20)"

9 (9, 10, 10)"

Chart A
Horseshoe cable (10 sts)

6
4
2
5
3
1

Chart B
Simple cable

8
6
4
2
7
5
3
1

4 sts

Chart C
Moss st

4
2
3
1

2-st rep   +1

Key

☐ St st (K on RS, P on WS)

▨ Rev St st (P on RS, K on WS)

RC: Place 2 sts on cn and hold
at back; K2, K2 from cn

LC: Place 2 sts on cn and hold
at front; K2, K2 from cn

Chart D

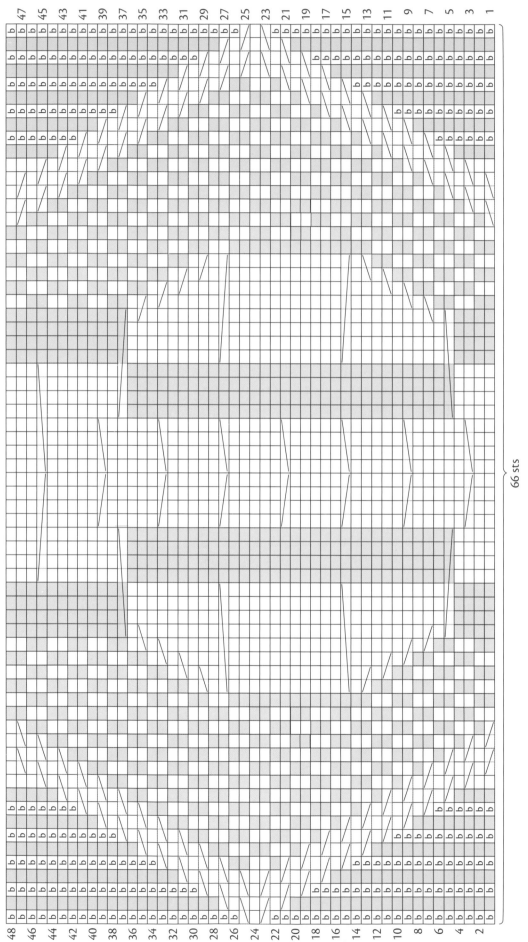

66 sts

Key

		St st (K on RS, P on WS)
		Rev St st (P on RS, K on WS)
b		Work into back of st
		Place 1 st on cn and hold at back; K1, K1 from cn
		Place 1 st on cn and hold at front; K1, K1 from cn
		RC: Place 2 sts on cn and hold at back; K2, K2 from cn
		LC: Place 2 sts on cn and hold at front; K2, K2 from cn
		Place 4 sts on cn and hold at back; K4, K4 from cn
		Place 4 sts on cn and hold at front; K4, K4 from cn
		Place 4 sts on cn and hold at back; K4, P4 from cn
		Place 4 sts on cn and hold at front; P4, K4 from cn

Useful Information

ABBREVIATIONS AND GLOSSARY

*	repeat the instructions following the asterisk as directed
approx	approximately
beg	begin(ning)
BO	bind off
cn	cable needle
CO	cast on
cont	continue(ing)
dec(s)	decrease(s)(ing)
dpn(s)	double pointed needle(s)
EOR	every other row
g	grams
garter st	garter stitch [knit every row]
inc(s)	increase(s)(ing)
K1b	knit into back of stitch
K2tog	knit 2 stitches together as one
mm	millimeter(s)
M1	make 1 stitch
oz	ounces
P2tog	purl 2 stitches together as one
P3tog	purl 3 stitches together as one
patt(s)	pattern(s)
pm	place marker
PU	pick up and knit
rem	remain(s)(ing)
rep(s)	repeat(s)
rnd(s)	round(s)
RS	right side
rev St st	reverse stockinette stitch [purl on right side, knit on wrong side]
sc	single crochet
sl	slip
ssk	slip, slip, knit [slip 1 stitch knitwise, slip 1 stitch knitwise, insert the left needle into the front of the two slipped stitches, knit the 2 stitches together as one]
st(s)	stitch(es)
St st	stockinette stitch [back and forth: knit on right side, purl on wrong side; in the round: knit every round]
tbl	through back loop
tog	together
WS	wrong side
yd(s)	yard(s)
YO(s)	yarn over(s)

METRIC CONVERSIONS

Yards x .91 = meters

Meters x 1.09 = yards

Grams x .035 = ounces

Ounces x 28.35 = grams

SKILL LEVEL

◖■□□◗ **Beginner:** Projects for first-time knitters using basic knit and purl stitches. Minimal shaping.

◖■■□◗ **Easy:** Project using basic stitches, repetitive stitch patterns, and simple color changes. Simple shaping and finishing.

◖■■■◗ **Intermediate:** Projects using a variety of stitches, such as basic cables and lace, simple intarsia, and techniques for double-pointed needles and knitting in the round. Mid-level shaping.

◖■■■◗ **Experienced:** Project using advanced techniques and stitches, such as short rows, Fair Isle, intricate intarsia, cables, lace patterns, and numerous color changes.

STANDARD YARN-WEIGHT SYSTEM

Yarn-Weight Symbol and Category Names	1 Super Fine	2 Fine	3 Light	4 Medium	5 Bulky	6 Super Bulky
Types of Yarns in Category	Sock, Fingering, Baby	Sport, Baby	DK, Light Worsted	Worsted, Afghan, Aran	Chunky, Craft, Rug	Bulky, Roving
Knit Gauge Ranges in Stockinette Stitch to 4"	27 to 32 sts	23 to 26 sts	21 to 24 sts	16 to 20 sts	12 to 15 sts	6 to 11 sts
Recommended Needle in U.S. Size Range	1 to 3	3 to 5	5 to 7	7 to 9	9 to 11	11 and larger
Recommended Needle in Metric Size Range	2.25 to 3.25 mm	3.25 to 3.75 mm	3.75 to 4.5 mm	4.5 to 5.5 mm	5.5 to 8 mm	8 mm and larger

RESOURCES

Contact the following companies to find shops
that carry the materials featured in this book.

Classic Elite Yarns
www.classiceliteyarns.com
Duchess, Montera, Princess, Renaissance, Waterlily

Dill Buttons
www.dill-buttons.com

Fiesta Yarns
www.fiestayarns.com
Kokopelli

Plymouth Yarns
www.plymouthyarn.com
Galway, Galway Highland, Plymouth Tweed

Russi Sales, Inc.
www.russisales.com
Chuckanut Bay Yarns

ABOUT THE AUTHOR

Certified as a Master Knitter, Sara is a member of the Association of Knitwear Designers and chairs the Learn to Knit program for The Knitting Guild Association. Her designs have been seen in numerous magazines and yarn company lines, and she has been published in several books as a contributing designer. Her Web site can be found at www.saraharper.com.

Sara lives in Virginia's Shenandoah Valley with her husband, a university professor, and their three children. When not occupying her time knitting, Sara enjoys spinning on an Ashford Elizabeth spinning wheel, quilting, gardening, reading, and caring for a house full of pets.

KNITTING AND CROCHET TITLES

KNITTING

200 Knitted Blocks

365 Knitting Stitches a Year: Perpetual Calendar

A to Z of Knitting

Blankets, Hats, and Booties

Double Exposure

Everyday Style

Fair Isle Sweaters Simplified

First Knits

Fun and Funky Knitting

Funky Chunky Knitted Accessories

Handknit Skirts

Handknit Style II

Kitty Knits—*New!*

Knit One, Stripe Too

Knits, Knots, Buttons, and Bows

Knitted Shawls, Stoles, and Scarves

The Knitter's Book of Finishing Techniques

Knitting Beyond the Basics

Knitting Circles around Socks

Knitting with Gigi

The Little Box of Knits for Baby

The Little Box of Knitted Gifts

The Little Box of Knitted Throws

The Little Box of Scarves II

The Little Box of Socks—*New!*

Modern Classics

More Sensational Knitted Socks

Ocean Breezes

The Pleasures of Knitting

Pursenalities

Pursenality Plus

Romantic Style

Saturday Sweaters

Sensational Knitted Socks

Silk Knits

Simple Gifts for Dog Lovers—*New!*

Special Little Knits from Just One Skein

Stitch Style: Mittens

Stitch Style: Socks

Stripes, Stripes, Stripes—*New!*

Too Cute!

Top Down Sweaters

Wrapped in Comfort

The Yarn Stash Workbook

CROCHET

365 Crochet Stitches a Year: Perpetual Calendar

Amigurumi World—*New!*

A to Z of Crochet—*New!*

Crochet for Tots

Crocheted Pursenalities

Crocheted Socks!

The Essential Book of Crochet Techniques

Eye-Catching Crochet

First Crochet

Fun and Funky Crochet

The Little Box of Crochet for Baby

The Little Box of Crocheted Bags

The Little Box of Crocheted Gifts

The Little Box of Crocheted Ponchos and Wraps

The Little Box of Crocheted Scarves

The Little Box of Crocheted Throws

Martingale®
& COMPANY

America's Best-Loved Craft & Hobby Books®
America's Best-Loved Knitting Books®

Our books are available at bookstores and your favorite craft, fabric, and yarn retailers. If you don't see the title you're looking for, visit us at **www.martingale-pub.com** or contact us at:

1-800-426-3126

International: 1-425-483-3313

Fax: 1-425-486-7596 • Email: info@martingale-pub.com